Light & Color Theory

Find the Light & Color of your aura and discover the deeper meaning behind each light and color of the Human Universe

RYAN HOSKINS

Christine Schmidt, Editor Paula Doubleday, Design & Layout

Contact & Follow Ryan

lightandcolortheory.com
ryan@lightandcolortheory.com

Light & Color Theory

www.instagram.com/lightandcolortheory

www.facebook.com/lightandcolortheory

www.lightandcolortheory.tumblr.com

Ryan Hoskins – Artist

www.instagram.com/ryanhoskinsartist

www.facebook.com/ryanhoskinsart

www.ryanhoskinsartist.tumblr.com

@ryanhoskinsart

www.linkedin.com/in/ryan-hoskins-2301a511a

© 2019 Ryan Hoskins. All rights reserved.

Contents

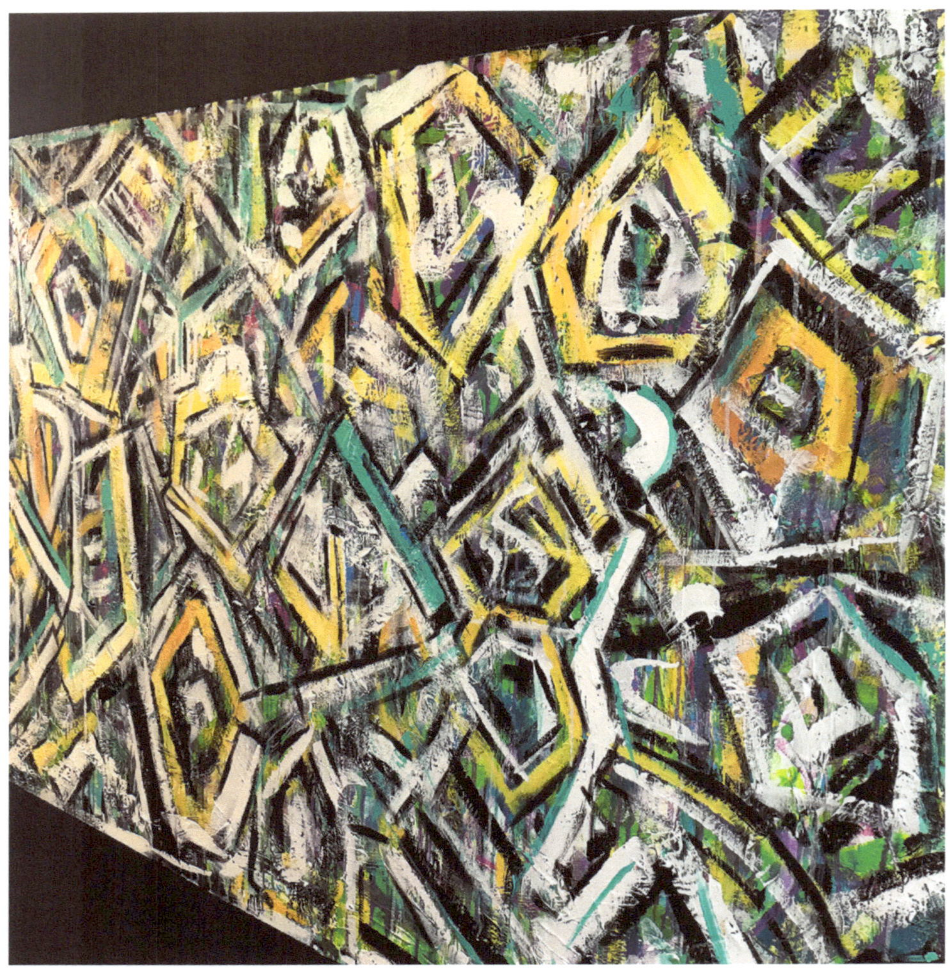

Out of Dark was the first painting I created after leaving my job to pursue art full time. It explores victory, reason, peace, power, acceptance, instinct, tolerance, and sacrifice.

Chapter 1

In the Garden

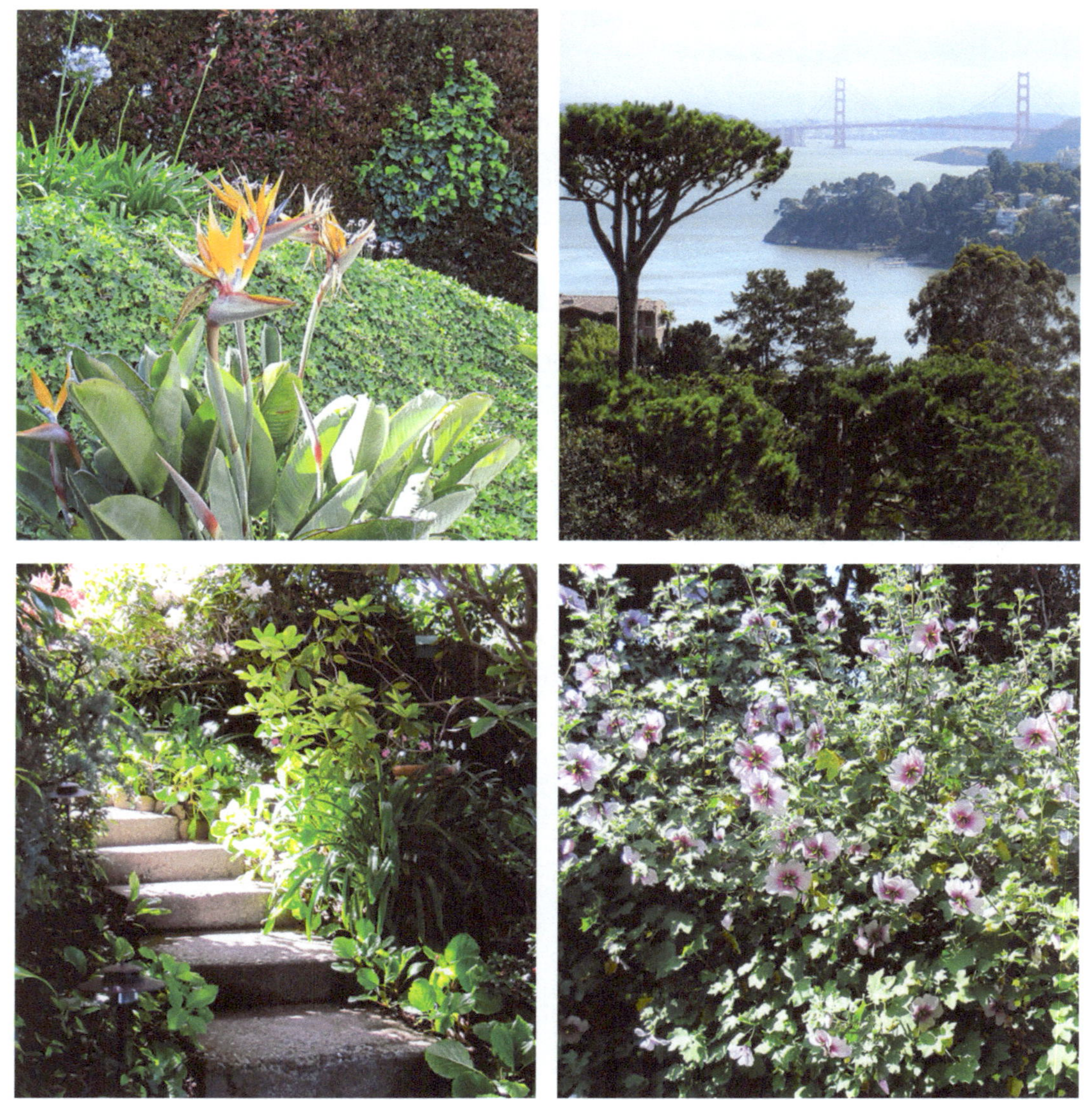

As a young child, I spent hours and hours adventuring in the garden. My companions were purple morning glories and fiery birds-of-paradise situated along gently sloping, ivy-covered hills. The golden loquat, red plum, and green apple trees offered me their affection, their soft leaves, and their juicy fruits. The Japanese maple and the Canadian maple competed for my attention in their own clever ways. It was the kaleidoscope of petunias, pansies, and cherry tomatoes that introduced me not just to what color looked like, but to what color felt like. The delicate pink roses, orange poppies, flashy purple-and-pink fuchsias, and intoxicating white jasmine all embodied their colors' persona. Towering pine trees, wondrous blue ivy, and peculiar mushrooms perched upon dark rich soils took the lights and the colors beyond their names and into real life.

Magnificent rainbows regularly adorned this little garden by the San Francisco Bay, and each season brought its own magic. Long summer evenings. Dark, cold, and rainy winters. Blustery, violent springs with a dazzling explosion of color at their hasty ends. Falls were calm and glistening accompanied by ice-cold fog after the final glimpse of the baking sun. I was outside no matter the weather. The lights and the colors that surrounded me were my friends. They were gentle, they kept me calm, and they kept me alive.

Chapter 2

An Introduction to Light & Color Theory

Light & Color Theory is first and foremost a conceptual art piece that aims to help people better understand themselves, others, and the Universe we all share. Imagine, for a second, that you have stumbled upon a small art museum in your town. Perhaps, a museum that you have never seen before. You walk through the rooms of this freshly discovered museum, presented with intriguing ideas and visual concepts about both yourself and the world. You decide to look a little deeper and find yourself opening up to growth, experiencing new joys, and having a sincere moment of relaxation.

This little pink book is an exhibit of Light & Color Theory, and it intends to offer unique perspectives on the world and to provide you with deep insights into yourself and others by using a dash of imagination. At its heart, it is designed to help you better understand yourself, your relationships, and the mysteries of our expanding and accelerating Universe. I hope you choose to enter this Light & Color exhibit and experience it in your own personal way.

Light & Color Theory first took root in a small garden by the San Francisco Bay. In the garden by the bay, I began to intuitively understand that each Light and that each Color represented a unique building block of our Universe, or Elemental Energy. In addition, I sensed that each Light and each Color tended to behave or act in a certain way, which I called their Primary Behavior Trait. The fundamental way in which each Light or Color tended to learn or experience the world, I called their Primary Comprehension Trait.

After leaving the garden, I began to recognize something remarkable in the people I met in my life. What I had observed in the garden was taking shape around me. It became more and more obvious to me that each person's Mind was a Light, that each person's Body was a Color, and that, together, the Light of the Mind and the Color of the Body worked in conjunction to create the Light & Color State of a person's Being.

It was clear to me that these three unique components (the Light of the Mind, the Color of the Body, and the Light & Color State of the Being) all worked in combination to create the aura surrounding the Human Body.

In addition to sensing the aura created by the Lights and Colors from the garden, I soon began to recognize the different influences of the Lights and Colors on the Human Body. The Light of the Mind, the Color of the Body, and the Light & Color State of the Being all affected the ways in which humans behaved in, and interpreted, the world around them. For some people, their Mind, their Body, and their Being were all the same Light and Color. For others, all 3 Light & Color Components were different.

In *Light & Color Theory*, you will see the most recent culmination of a lifelong effort to explain and elaborate upon the wisdom of the Lights and Colors that I first encountered in the garden. *Light & Color Theory* will foster your imagination, spark intriguing dialogue, and often bring a smile to your face.

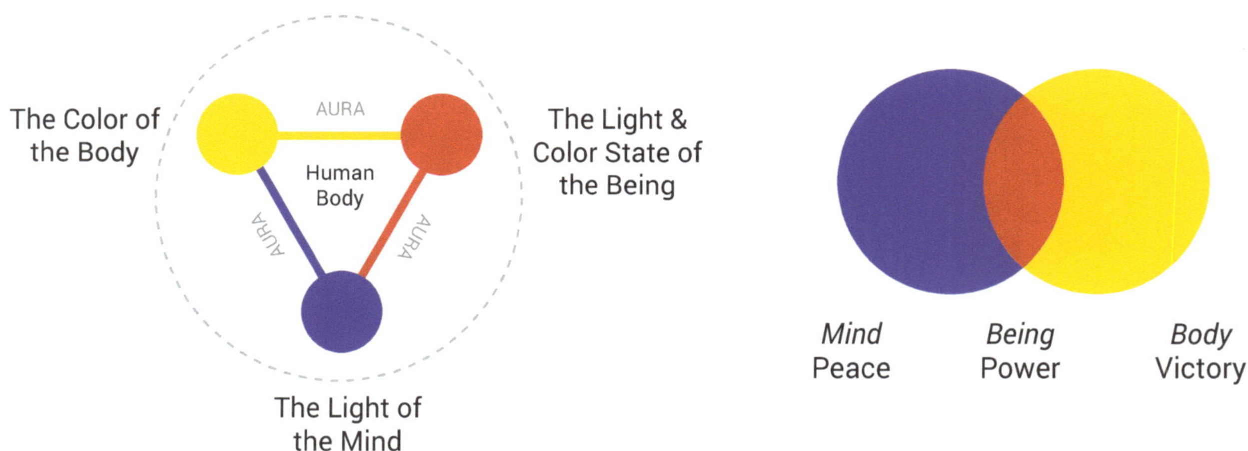

At the very least, I want you to enjoy it—take the things you like and leave the rest. You may learn valuable ideas helpful for internal reflection, or you may simply be entertained by taking the quiz with your friends and finding out the 3 Light & Color Components of your aura. One thing I know for sure is that we all experience a great deal of happiness when we feel present and connected to the moment at hand.

With *Light & Color Theory*, you can learn to cherish the Lights and Colors that surround you all the time. You can become more deeply interested in the visual world, the spiritual world, and feel more connected to yourself, others, and the Universe.

And one last thing . . . it is important to know that each Light and each Color is eternally beautiful and eternally valuable.

Chapter 3

The 7 Principles of Light & Color Theory

After years of observing Light, Color, and human behavior, I began to explore my thoughts and ideas by creating Light & Color Theory. During this process, I identified 7 principles that shaped and formed its basic foundation. They are as follows:

1. There are 9 different Lights and there are 9 different Colors in the Human Universe.
2. Each of the 9 Lights and each of the 9 Colors has 1 of 3 Primary Behavior Traits and 1 of 3 Primary Comprehension Traits.
3. Each of the 9 Lights and each of the 9 Colors signifies 1 of the 9 Elemental Energies that comprise the Human Universe.
4. Every person's Mind is a Light.
5. Every person's Body is a Color.
6. The Light of the Mind shines onto the Color of the Body to form the Light & Color State of the Being.
7. Each person has 3 Light & Color Components that work together to form their aura: The Light of the Mind, the Color of the Body, and the Light & Color State of the Being. All 3 Light & Color Components affect the ways in which human beings behave in, and interpret, the world around them. For some people, all 3 components of their aura will be the same Light and Color. For others, all 3 components will be different Lights and Colors.

Chapter 4

The Basics of Each Light & Color

In Chapter 4, we will dissect the basics of each Light and of each Color. Let's start our journey with **Principle 1: There are 9 different Lights and there are 9 different Colors in the Human Universe.** The first Light of the Human Universe is Black Light (1), or the state of "No Light," the absence of Light. The first Color of the Human Universe is White Color (1), or the state of "No Color," the absence of Color. The second state of both Light and Color is Red (2), followed by Orange (3), then Yellow (4), then Green (5), then Blue (6), then Purple (7), then Pink (8). The ninth and final Light of the Human Universe is White Light (9), or the state of "All Light." The ninth and final Color of the Human Universe is Black Color or the state of "All Color." These are the 9 Lights and Colors that define the Human Universe.

PRINCIPLE 1

There are 9 different Lights and there are 9 different Colors in the Human Universe.

LIGHTS	COLORS
1. Black Light (No Light)	1. White Color (No Color)
2. Red Light	2. Red Color
3. Orange Light	3. Orange Color
4. Yellow Light	4. Yellow Color
5. Green Light	5. Green Color
6. Blue Light	6. Blue Color
7. Purple Light	7. Purple Color
8. Pink Light	8. Pink Color
9. White Light (All Light)	9. Black Color (All Color)

Now that we know the 9 Lights and the 9 Colors of the Human Universe, let's take a closer look at the Primary Traits of each Light and of each Color by examining Principle 2.

PRINCIPLE 2

Each of the 9 Lights and each of the 9 Colors has 1 of 3 Primary Behavior Traits and 1 of 3 Primary Comprehension Traits.

In the garden, I observed that each Light and Color had 1 of 3 **Primary Behavior Traits**. I define the Primary Behavior Trait as the fundamental way in which each Light or each Color tended to behave or act. For instance, the Blue sky was trustworthy and reliable, while the Yellow loquats strived for originality. The Primary Behavior Traits that I discovered in the garden were:

Confidence

A self-assurance arising from an appreciation of abilities or qualities

Creativity

An ability to effectively use imagination and original ideas

Responsibility

The capacity to be trusted or relied upon

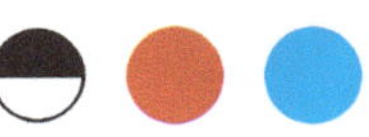

In addition, I observed in the garden that each Light and each Color had 1 of 3 **Primary Comprehension Traits**. I define the Primary Comprehension Trait as the fundamental way in which each Light or each Color tends to learn or perceive the world. For example, the Red rose was always available for a friendly hello, while the Orange wildflowers had a high need for sensibility. The Primary Comprehension Traits that I found in the garden were:

Positivity

The practice of being present and optimistic in attitude

Intuition

The ability to understand without the need for conscious reasoning

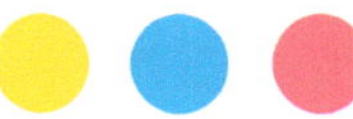

Logic

The ability to be perceptive and sensible given the circumstances

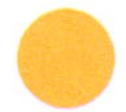
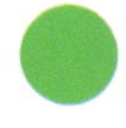

Below is a Light & Color Reference Chart illustrating the Primary Behavior Trait and Primary Comprehension Trait for each of the 9 Lights and Colors.

Light/Color	Primary Behavior	Primary Comprehension
Black/White	Responsibility	Logic
Red	Responsibility	Positivity
Orange	Confidence	Logic
Yellow	Creativity	Intuition
Green	Creativity	Logic
Blue	Responsibility	Intuition
Purple	Confidence	Positivity
Pink	Confidence	Intuition
White/Black	Creativity	Positivity

PRINCIPLE 3

Each of the 9 Lights and each of the 9 Colors signifies 1 of the 9 Elemental Energies that comprise the Human Universe.

To finish chapter 4, let's examine Principle 3. Back in the garden, I also found that each Light and each Color had a unique **Elemental Energy** deep within itself. By observing the Primary Behavior Trait in combination with the Primary Comprehension Trait of each Light and of each Color, I began to understand the Elemental Energy that each of the Lights and Colors contained.

For example, Red Light and Color, with its fierce accountability and determined presence, was the essence of Power. Blue Light and Color, with its yearning for commitment and acute sensitivity, was the epitome of Tolerance. Below is a list of each Light and Color and their Primary Behavior Trait, Primary Comprehension Trait, and Elemental Energy.

Light/Color	Primary Behavior	Primary Comprehension	Elemental Energy
Black/White	Responsibility	Logic	Instinct
Red	Responsibility	Positivity	Power
Orange	Confidence	Logic	Dominance
Yellow	Creativity	Intuition	Victory
Green	Creativity	Logic	Reason
Blue	Responsibility	Intuition	Tolerance
Purple	Confidence	Positivity	Peace
Pink	Confidence	Intuition	Sacrifice
White/Black	Creativity	Positivity	Acceptance

Chapter 5

Finding the Light & Color of Your Aura

The Light & Color of your aura is something you may know subconsciously but have yet to truly discover. Even as a young child, the Light of your Mind shined onto the Color of your Body to form the Light & Color State of your Being – all 3 components creating the full picture of your aura.

The Light & Color of your aura consists of 3 Components:

1. The Light of Your Mind

2. The Color of Your Body

3. Light & Color State of Your Being

All 3 Light & Color Components affect the way you behave in, and interpret, the world around you. Taking the Light & Color Quiz, which can be found in Chapter 6, starts with reviewing Principles 4, 5, and 6 of Light & Color Theory.

PRINCIPLE 4

Every person's Mind is a Light.

Every person's Mind is a Light, and it is the first component of our aura. The Light of your Mind is the Elemental Energy that you most want to see in the world, and therefore, you do your best to shine that force into the world.

Our Minds are born with a predominant, but tiny, Light. While we often maintain and grow the Light we are born with, we do get the chance to change our Light at certain crucial times throughout our lives. These periods often align with an astrological concept known as Saturn return and occur every 27–30 years. Saturn return is when the planet Saturn returns to your natal Saturn, or the position in which Saturn was in when you were born. For more information on Saturn return, check out the work of author and astrologer Suzanne White.

PRINCIPLE 5

Every person's Body is a Color.

Every person's Body is a Color, and it is the second component of our aura. For humans, our Body Color is the one Light that we do not absorb.

Physics teaches that the Color of any object we see is actually the Color of the "light" that the object is not absorbing. For example, when we see a Red object, like a tomato, we are seeing an object with a chemical composition that absorbs every Light except for Red. When a tomato is hit with the White Light of the sun, it absorbs the Orange, Yellow, Green, Blue, Purple, and Pink Lights. Red Light, however, is not absorbed by the tomato, and is instead reflected back into the Universe—and that is what we see, the unabsorbed Red Light.

Since our Body Color is the one Light that we do not absorb, just like the tomato, a person with a Red Body will absorb every Light except for Red. To compensate for this, our Body desires and creates that missing Elemental Energy for us.

We are born with the Color of our Body, whose final hue settles in around puberty.

PRINCIPLE 6

The Light of the Mind shines onto the Color of the Body to form the Light & Color State of the Being.

The final component of our aura is the Light & Color State of our Being. The Light & Color State of the Being arises from the Light of the Mind shining across the Color of the Body, revealing the final Elemental Energy that our aura contains. Interestingly, through the study of physics, we have also learned that different Lights and different Colors interact to form new Light & Color States. For instance, when you shine a Purple Light onto a Yellow object, the Yellow object turns to Red Color. This is because the Yellow object is reflecting both the Red and Green Lights of the sun.

When adding Light, Red Light and Green Light add together to form Yellow Light. When we shine a Purple Light onto a Yellow object, the Yellow object is now isolated in a state where only Red Light and Blue Light exist. The Blue Light is absorbed by the object, the Red Light is still reflected, but now there is no longer any Green Light for the object to reflect. Since the Yellow object can no longer reflect any Green Light, it now appears to be only Red in Color.

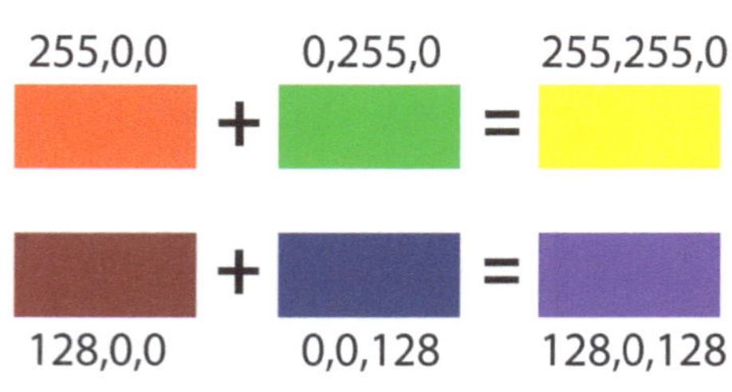

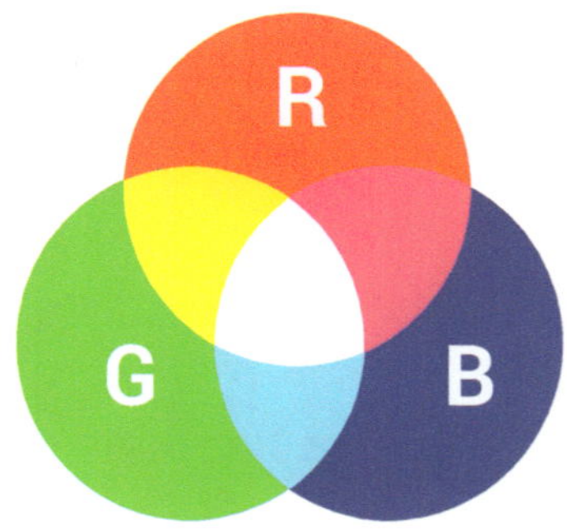

The Light of our Mind and the Color of our Body act in the same way. A person with a Yellow Body and a Purple Mind will have a Red Light & Color State of the Being. Working together, the Light of the Mind, the Color of the Body, and the Light & Color State of the Being all create the aura—the forces of Light and Color that show us the Elemental Energies that comprise our Human Body.

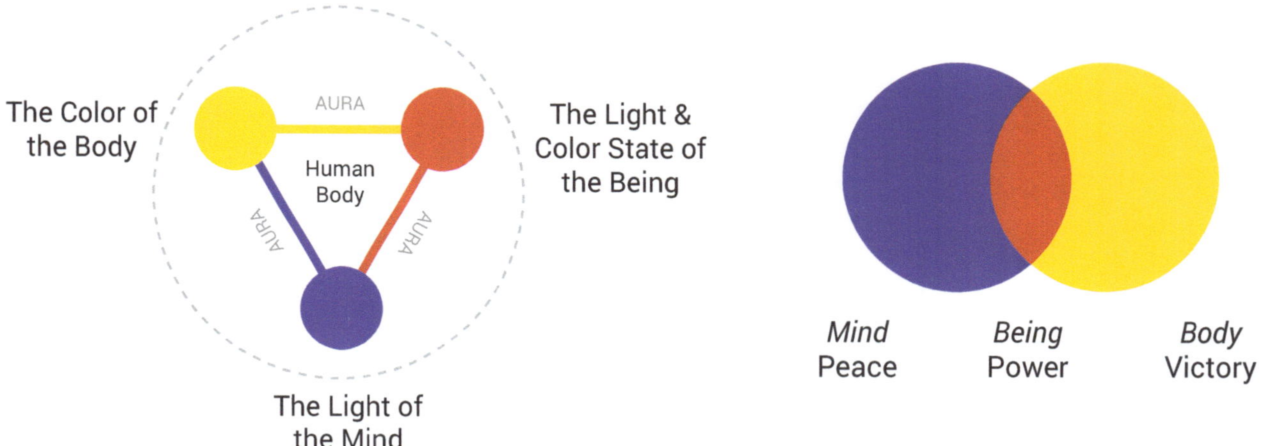

Finding the Light & Color of Your Aura

You can find the Light & Color of your aura in two easy steps.

1. First, use the Light & Color Quiz in Chapter 6 to find the Light of your Mind and the Color of your Body.
2. Next, use the Light & Color Charts, which follow the quiz, to see how the Light of your Mind and the Color of your Body interact to form the Light & Color State of your Being.

As you see in the Light & Color Chart below, you will be one of 81 unique Light & Color Combinations (Aura Types) consisting of 3 Light & Color Components.

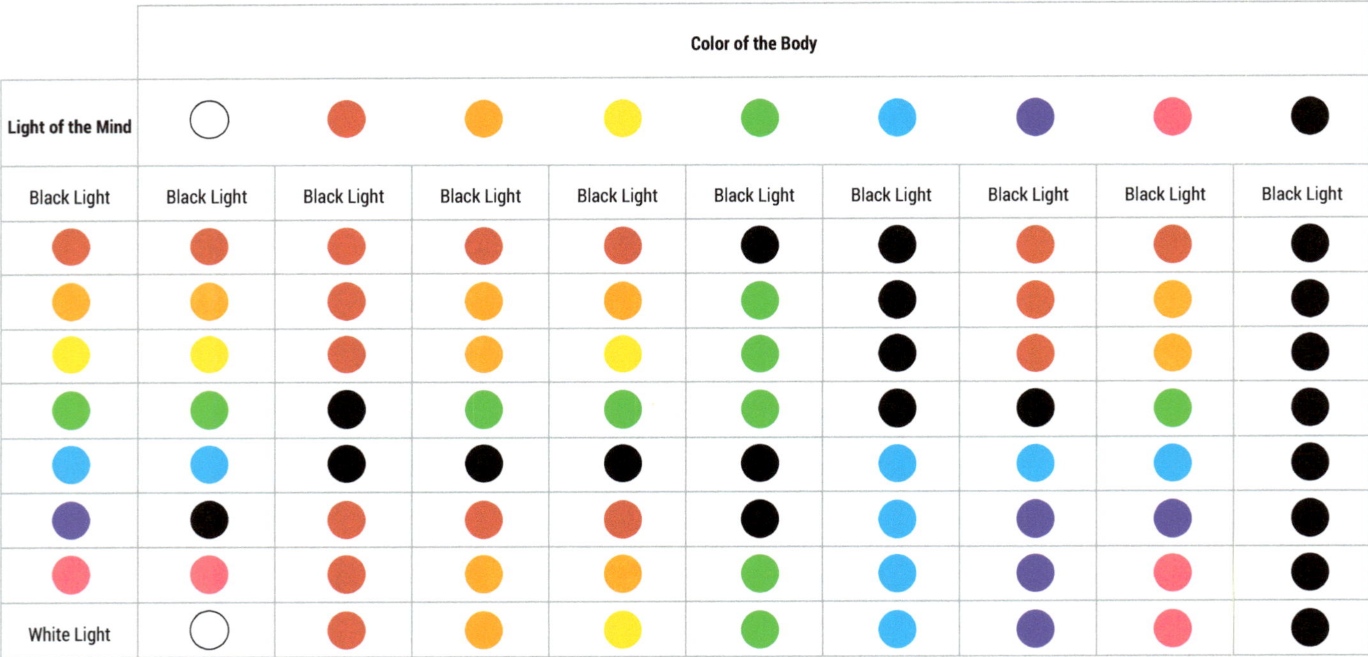

In Chapter 7, we will cover Principle 7 of Light & Color Theory and investigate how each of the 3 Light & Color Components of your aura inspires your thinking and behavior. Now it's time to take the quiz!

Chapter 6

The Light & Color Quiz

The Light & Color Theory Quiz deciphers the Primary Behavior Trait (Confident, Creative, or Responsible) and Primary Comprehension Trait (Positive, Intuitive, or Logical) of both your Mind and Body. For the quiz, we have chosen to examine the Mind and the Body when they are feeling their happiest and at their best, because it is easiest for our Lights and Colors to shine through when we are happy and enjoying the world.

Take a moment to breathe and relax. Think about where your Mind and your Body are at their happiest and at their best. It could be different places; it could be the same place. I will use myself as an example after each section of the quiz so you can better understand how it works. There is no need for worry or hesitation. Your personal Light & Color will shine through.

The Light & Color Quiz

What Light is My Mind?

In this portion of the quiz, we are deciphering the Primary Behavior Trait and Primary Comprehension Trait of your Mind. Choose one of the answers from each of the following two groups. Choose the answer you believe is most like you when your Mind is happiest and at its best. Often the best answer is the one that feels most correct after reading it out loud.

Group I – Primary Behavior Traits

The fundamental way in which my Mind tends to behave or act when it's at its best and happiest is:

1. **Confident.** My Mind has self-assurance arising from an appreciation of my abilities or my qualities. My Mind takes life head-on. My Mind determines its own course. My Mind wants to do something big. My Mind works hard and plays hard. My Mind likes to win.
2. **Creative.** My Mind has the ability to effectively use imagination and original ideas. My Mind likes to be itself. My Mind has unique perspectives and ideas.
3. **Responsible.** My Mind has the capacity to be trusted or relied upon. My Mind enjoys being accountable and active. My Mind is comfortable sacrificing for others. My Mind relaxes when all the work is done.

Group II – Primary Comprehension Traits

The fundamental way in which my Mind tends to learn or experience the world when it's at its best and happiest is:

A. **Positive.** My Mind is present and optimistic. My Mind is always looking for the best in each situation. My Mind is easily enthused and can occupy itself. My Mind enjoys connecting with others and sharing in happiness.

B. **Intuitive.** My Mind has the ability to understand something without the need for conscious reasoning. My Mind is clear on when I am comfortable and like something. My Mind enjoys knowing who and what it can trust. My Mind is comfortable with empathy, both receiving and giving it. My Mind enjoys understanding other people.

C. **Logical.** My Mind has the ability to be perceptive and sensible given the circumstances. My Mind enjoys getting the work done, but it likes to work alone. My Mind is efficient and perfectionistic. When analyzing a situation, my Mind prefers to concentrate on facts instead of feelings. My Mind does not let emotions interfere with what is important. My Mind does not display weakness.

Now I'll use myself as an example. My Mind feels its *happiest* and at its *best* while I'm out with my friends—my Mind is confident and positive when I am talking with my friends and having a good time. My Mind feels self-assured, and it is extremely present and focused on the moment at hand. Therefore, for me, the Primary Behavior Trait of my Mind is Confidence and the Primary Comprehension Trait of my Mind is Positivity.

After picking your answers from each group on the previous two pages, combine your number from the first group with your letter from the second group to uncover the Light of your Mind. For example, if you are Responsible (3) and Intuitive (B), your Mind is Blue Light (3B).

The Light of Your Mind is:

Black light	3C
Red light	3A
Orange light	1C
Yellow light	2B
Green light	2C
Blue light	3B
Purple light	1A
Pink light	1B
White light	2A

What Color is My Body?

In the second portion of the quiz, we are deciphering the Primary Behavior Trait and Primary Comprehension Trait of your Body. Choose one answer from each of the following two groups just like you did for your Mind. Choose the answer you believe is the most like you when your Body is happiest and at its best. Often the best answer is the one that feels most correct after reading it out loud.

Group I – Primary Behavior Traits

The fundamental way in which my Body tends to behave or act when it's at its best and happiest is:

1. **Confident.** My Body has self-assurance arising from an appreciation of my abilities or my qualities. My Body takes life head on. My Body likes to be in charge. My Body wants to achieve something big. My Body likes to work hard and play hard. My Body enjoys winning.
2. **Creative.** My Body has the ability to effectively use imagination and original ideas. My body enjoys being rhythmic and fun. My body is always coming up with creative ideas or places to be. My Body does not feel the need to move all the time—it is okay for it to rest.
3. **Responsible.** My Body has the capacity to be trusted and relied upon. My Body likes being proactive. My Body is willing to make sacrifices for others. My Body feels comfortable once all the work is done.

Group II – Primary Comprehension Traits

The fundamental way in which my Body tends to learn or experience the world when it's at its best and happiest is:

A. **Positive.** My Body is present and optimistic. My Body always believes things will work out for the best. My Body is easily enthused by new things. My Body is never bored. My Body enjoys socializing and sharing in happiness.

B. **Intuitive.** My Body has the ability to understand something without the need for conscious reasoning. My Body knows what it enjoys. My Body feels most comfortable when it knows who and what it can trust. My Body likes to understand others.

C. **Logical.** My Body has the ability to be perceptive or sensible given the circumstances. My Body is patient. My Body likes to keep emotions cool and logical. My Body craves perfectionism and prefers to work alone. When analyzing a situation, my Body prefers to focus on facts. My Body does not display weakness. My Body knows how to get results, regardless of the situation.

Using myself as an example again, my Body feels its *happiest* and at its *best*—creative and logical—when I am painting or playing golf. It's always coming up with unique ideas and then exploring them through rigorous processes. Therefore, for my Body, its Primary Behavior Trait is Creativity and its Primary Comprehension Trait is Logic.

After picking your answers from the previous two pages, combine your number from Group I with your letter from Group II to uncover the Color of your Body. For example, if you are Creative (2) and Positive (A), your Body is Black Color (2A).

The Color of Your Body is:

White color	3C
Red color	3A
Orange color	1C
Yellow color	2B
Green color	2C
Blue color	3B
Purple color	1A
Pink color	1B
Black color	2A

Light & Color State of the Being

Now that you have taken the Light & Color Quiz, you know the Light of your Mind and the Color of your Body. As we learned in Principle 6, the Light & Color State of the Being is formed by the Light of the Mind shining onto the Color of the Body—essentially the intersection of Mind and Body.

Here is a brief example of a Purple Light Mind intersecting with a Green Color Body. If you have a Green Color Body, you have a Body that reflects Green Light and absorbs all other Lights. When you place a Green Color Body in a state where there is only Purple Light, there is no Green Light for the Body to reflect, and the Purple Light is still absorbed. So, the Body now appears to be Black because it is absorbing all Light. We live in a world with all 9 Lights, but when we are looking at the Light & Color State of the Being, it's like looking at the Body in a world where the only Light that exists is the Light of the Mind—in this case, Purple Light.

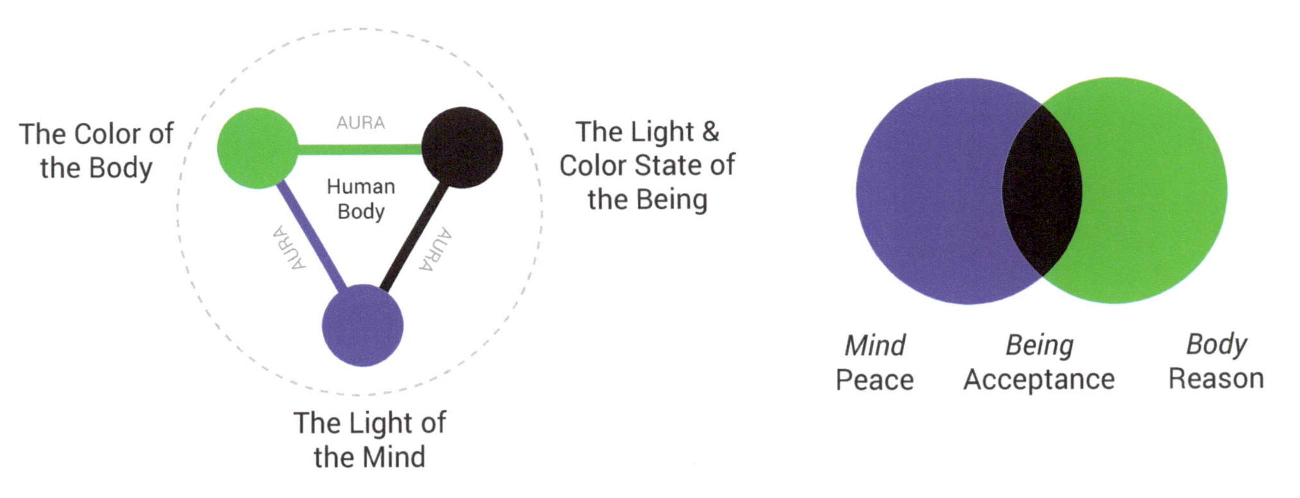

Find your Light & Color State of the Being where your Light of the Mind (left column) and the Color of your Body (top row) intersect in the chart below.

Light of the Mind	Color of the Body								
Black Light	Black Light	Black Light	Black Light	Black Light	Black Light	Black Light	Black Light	Black Light	Black Light
Red Light	Red	Red	Red	Red	Black	Black	Red	Red	Black
Orange Light	Orange	Red	Orange	Orange	Green	Black	Red	Orange	Black
Yellow Light	Yellow	Red	Orange	Yellow	Green	Black	Red	Orange	Black
Green Light	Green	Black	Green	Green	Green	Black	Black	Green	Black
Blue Light	Blue	Black	Black	Black	Black	Blue	Blue	Blue	Black
Purple Light	Purple	Red	Red	Red	Black	Blue	Purple	Purple	Black
Pink Light	Pink	Red	Orange	Orange	Green	Blue	Purple	Pink	Black
White Light	White	Red	Orange	Yellow	Green	Blue	Purple	Pink	Black

Fill in your Lights and Colors:

Color of My Body	
Light of My Mind	
Light & Color of My State of the Being	

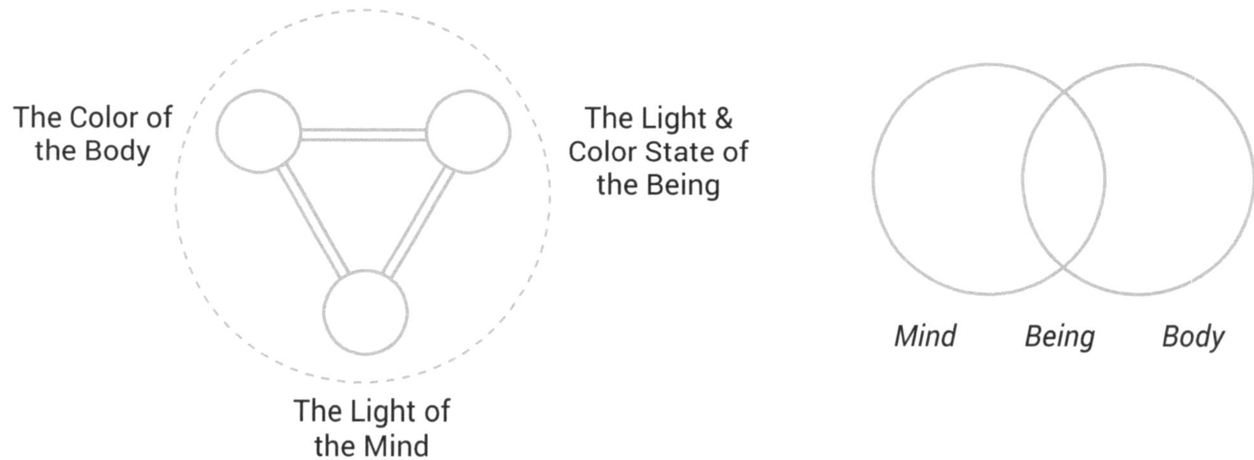

Chapter 7

Understanding the Light & Color of Your Aura

In this chapter, we will take a closer look at Principle 7 of Light & Color Theory and examine the ways in which each Light and each Color affect human behavior.

How Your Light & Color Affect Your Behavior

PRINCIPLE 7

Each person has 3 Light & Color Components that work together to form their aura: The Light of the Mind, the Color of the Body, and the Light & Color State of the Being. All 3 Light & Color Components affect the ways in which human beings behave in, and interpret, the world around them. For some people, all 3 components of their aura will be the same Light and Color. For others, all 3 components will be different Lights and Colors.

The Light of the Mind, the Color of the Body, and the Light & Color State of the Being all work together to form your aura. These 3 Light & Color Components affect how you behave in, and interpret, your world. Some people have the same Light & Color for all 3 components while others have different ones.

Each of the 9 Lights & Colors has a unique way of inspiring and shaping the Mind, the Body, and the Being. Their influence across the Mind, Body, and Being create a unique set of human characteristics, desires, and behaviors that help illuminate our world.

Now that you have taken the Light & Color Quiz and examined the Light & Color Charts, you should know all 3 Light & Color Components of your aura: the Light of your Mind, the Color of your Body, and the Light & Color State of your Being. Below is an illustration of the Light & Color Composition of the aura.

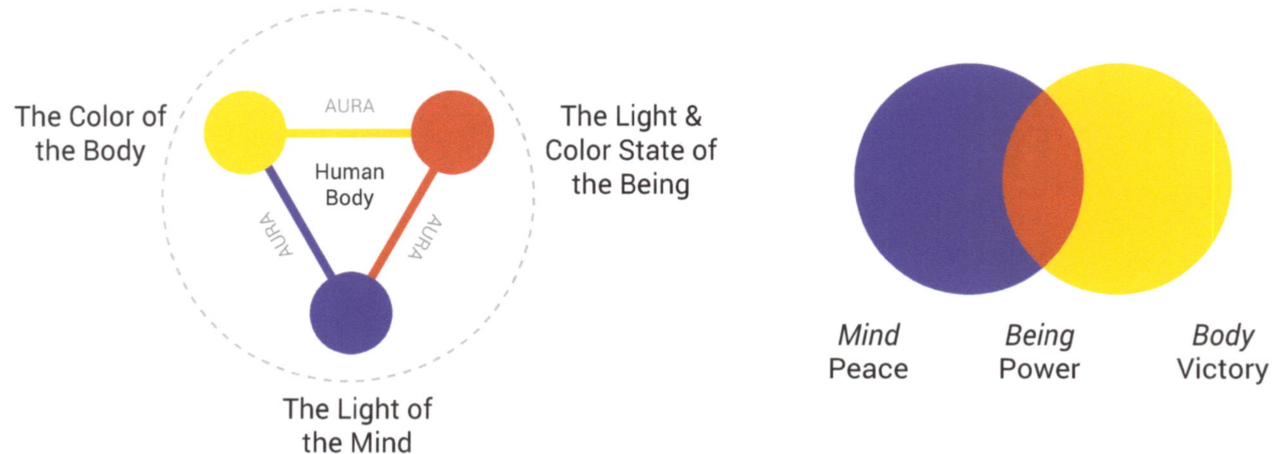

To see how each of your 3 Light & Color Components inspire you, take a look at their descriptions in the following overview of the nine components. For instance, if you have a Yellow Mind, a Purple Body, and a Red Being, you will want to read the Yellow, Purple, and Red component sections.

It is the elegant combination of our 3 Light & Color Components working together that illuminates the true essence of our Human Body—our current Terrestrial Vessel.

Generally speaking, you should exhibit approximately **80%** of the characteristics of your Light or Color Component. No one is every aspect of their Light or Color Component, as there are so many different shades of each Light and each Color. If you feel very close to a Light or Color Component, but are not that Light or Color Component, you may have had a parent, friend, or lover with that particular Light or Color.

Index of Light & Color Components

1. Black Light and White Color Component (Instinct Component)
2. Red Component (Power Component)
3. Orange Component (Dominance Component)
4. Yellow Component (Victory Component)
5. Green Component (Reason Component)
6. Blue Component (Tolerance Component)
7. Purple Component (Peace Component)
8. Pink Component (Sacrifice Component)
9. White Light and Black Color Component (Acceptance Component)

1
Black Light & White Color

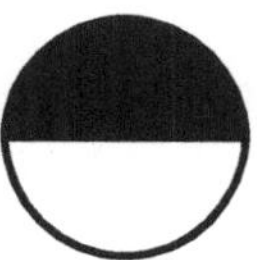

1

Deep Dive: Black Light and White Color

Instinct

The Elemental Energy that asserts itself when there is Black Light or White Color is Instinct.
Black Light and White Color are comprised of:

Primary Behavior Trait: **Responsibility** | Primary Comprehension Trait: **Logic**

BRIGHT

Survival

The bright side of Instinct is Survival:

Without any instinct, survival is impossible.

Endurance, Guts, Reality, Vitality, Permanence, Essence

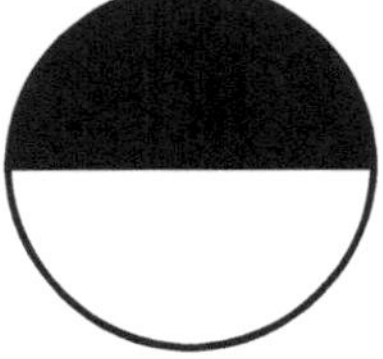

DARK

Violence

The dark side of Instinct is Violence:

The unwarranted use of temporary but destructive mental and physical forces against others and oneself.

Struggle, Bloodshed, Duress

People with an Instinct Component are serious people who are honest, objective, and conscience-oriented. They are inspired by principles and ideals and often strive for a higher purpose. They hate making mistakes and often have a strong mission in life. They must avoid anger, and they must be seen as "good" in order to feel loved.

Their worst childhood influence was the belief that "it's not okay to make mistakes." It is okay to make mistakes—it's how we learn. People containing Black Light or White Color also fear becoming bad or evil but should learn to let go of this fear. This will happen for them when they let go of their deepest belief that "you are good if you do what is right." They must learn that both they and others can be good, even if it feels like they're doing everything wrong.

People with Black Light and White Color Components often get lost in their search for perfection. Not everything has to be right—it is impossible to correct the unfolding Universe at every turn. People with Black Light and White Color must learn that their version of right and wrong is not everyone's version of right and wrong. And that fact is perfectly okay.

Their most important body part is the feet. Foot massages and walking on soft surfaces like beaches, trails in the woods, and grass can have great benefits for them.

Attributes:

- A serious, no-nonsense person
- Honest, objective, conscience-oriented
- Better safe than sorry
- Likes to have fun and should do it more often
- Inspired by principles and ideals
- Organized, responsible
- Has a mission in life

Potential weaknesses:

- Hates mistakes
- Loves defining right and wrong
- Overly burdened
- High standards
- Perfectionistic
- Judgmental

Must avoid:	Anger/wrath
Worst childhood influence:	It is not okay to make mistakes.
Fears becoming:	Bad or evil
Wants to be:	Good
Gets lost in:	Perfectionism
Should strive to:	Live for a greater purpose
Greatest evil:	Believing others must share in their vision of right and wrong
Avoid the negative of:	Yellow (moody, irrational)
Embrace the positive of:	Purple (joyous, spontaneous)
Deepest belief:	You are good if you do what is right.
Body part:	Feet
Famous people:	
Hillary Clinton	Martha Stewart
Plato	Henry David Thoreau

2
Red Light & Color

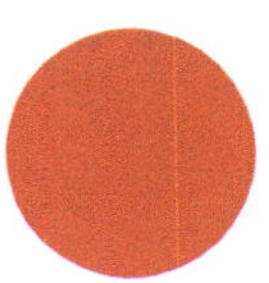

2

Deep Dive: Red Light & Color

Power

The Elemental Energy that asserts itself when there is Red Light or Red Color is Power.
Red Light and Red Color are comprised of:

Primary Behavior Trait: **Responsibility** | Primary Comprehension Trait: **Positivity**

BRIGHT

Giving

The bright side of Power is Giving:

Using one's power to fortify and protect others.

Guard, Uphold, Secure, Shield, Reinforce

DARK

Taking

The dark side of Power is Taking:

Using one's power to attack or transgress against others.

Assault, Rape, Resentful Displeasure, Break, War, Torture

People with a Red Component have the Elemental Energy of Power. They are friendly, talkative, and have a genuine concern for others. They express their emotions freely and are fierier than people expect. They are also capable of healing broken hearts. Reds must feel wanted in order to feel loved. They must avoid pride—it's not that they think they are the best but rather that they are injured and may not tell anyone. Sometimes they will rush into too much responsibility without thinking through the consequences.

Their worst childhood influence was the belief that "it's not okay to have your own needs." However, it is, of course, important and desirable to understand and fulfill our true needs. Reds often fear becoming unworthy of love. This will disappear as soon as they let go of their deepest belief that "you are good or okay if you are loved." They must learn that both they and others can be good even if they are not loved. Reds often get lost in the desire to be needed, often giving too much and then feeling used or rejected. They must learn to take care of themselves and then others. Reds must avoid using other people's needs and desires against them. Sometimes Reds will play with people's emotions in order to get what they want.

Their most important body part is the coccyx located at the base of the spine. According to my research, I've found that walking, singing, bicycling, dancing, and practicing the splits are excellent activities for Reds. They may see benefits from yellow foods like bananas, mangoes, and corn. They may also enjoy cooked tomatoes.

Attributes:

- Has a genuine concern for others
- Involved, friendly, talkative
- People like their attention and encouragement
- Deep desire to protect and nurture what they love
- Thoughtful, generous, compassionate, supportive
- Can express their emotions freely
- Can heal broken hearts
- Welcoming and appreciative of people

Potential weaknesses:

- Overly self-sacrificing
- Fierier than people expect
- Like to be giving, but wants it to be appreciated
- Want the affection of others, even to their own detriment
- Make an excessive effort to be close to people or control people

Must avoid: Pride

Worst childhood influence: It's not okay to have your own needs.

Fears becoming: Unworthy of love

Wants to be: Wanted

Gets lost in: The desire to be needed

Should strive to: Take care of themselves and others

Greatest evil: Using others needs and desires against them

Avoid the negative of: Pink (aggressive, dominating)

Embrace the positive of: Yellow (self-nourishing, emotionally aware)

Deepest belief: You are good if you are loved.

Body part: Coccyx

Famous people:

Mother Teresa	Florence Nightingale
Taylor Swift	Tiger Woods

3
Orange Light & Color

3

Deep Dive: Orange Light & Color

Dominance

The Elemental Energy that asserts itself when there is Orange Light or Orange Color is Dominance.
Orange Light and Orange Color are comprised of:

Primary Behavior Trait: **Confidence** | Primary Comprehension Trait: **Logic**

BRIGHT

Achievement

The bright side of Dominance is Achievement:

Using one's dominance to accomplish great deeds.

Create, Orgasm, Success, Effort, Feat

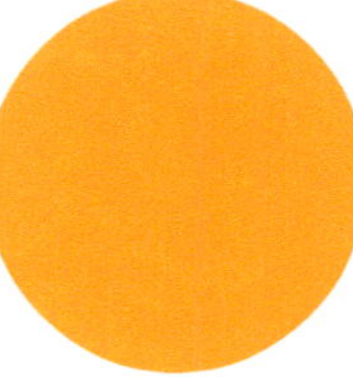

DARK

Oppression

The dark side of Dominance is Oppression:

Using one's dominance to control and abuse others.

Cruelty, Abuse, Suffering, Coercion, Molest

People with an Orange Component have the Elemental Energy of Dominance. They are efficient, effective, and competent. They make excellent first impressions and have the ability to "keep up with the neighbors." They are often highly adaptable, goal-focused, and extremely hard workers. Oranges must feel admired in order to feel loved. They must avoid vanity and the deception of themselves or others. Oranges must remember that they can only play a role for so long.

Their worst childhood influence was that "it's not okay to have feelings." Actually, feelings are the basis of happiness and human connection. They are important and need to be expressed and understood. Oranges fear becoming worthless. This will be cured when Oranges let go of their deepest belief that "you are good if you are liked and successful." Oranges must learn that both they and others can be good even if they are not liked and successful. Oranges can get lost chasing success. Instead, they should strive to develop themselves and then lead by example.

Their most important body part is the hips. I've found that bicycling, tennis, sex, and playing with animals are great for Oranges. They may also benefit from experiencing Blue things like blueberries or staring at the ocean.

Attributes:

- Competent, efficient, effective
- Glow when things are going well for them
- Make good first impressions
- Polite, well-mannered, friendly
- Adaptable, goal-focused

Potential weaknesses:

- Workaholic
- Can be cool, insecure, aloof
- High need for recognition and reward
- May try to cut corners in order to win
- Wants to be the best or nothing at all
- Important to be successful, even at great cost
- Tries to conceal insecurities and flaws

Must avoid: Deception

Worst childhood message: It's not okay to have feelings.

Fears becoming: Worthless

Wants to be: Admired for who they are

Gets lost in: Chasing success

Should strive to: Develop themselves and to lead by example

Greatest evil: Influencing others with deception

Avoid the negative of: Black Color/White light (apathetic)

Embrace the positive of: Blue (cooperative, committed to others)

Deepest belief: You are good if you are liked and successful.

Body part: Hips

Famous people:

F. Scott Fitzgerald
Rickie Fowler
Oprah Winfrey
Ariana Grande
Donald Trump

4
Yellow Light & Color

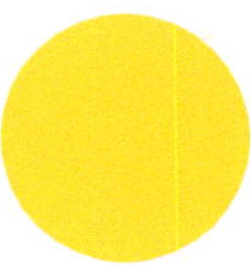

4

Deep Dive: Yellow Light & Color

Victory

The Elemental Energy that asserts itself when there is Yellow Light or Yellow Color is Victory. Yellow Light and Color are comprised of:

Primary Behavior Trait: **Creativity** | Primary Comprehension Trait: **Intuition**

BRIGHT

Individualism

The bright side of Victory is Individualism:

The freedom to be independent and self-reliant.

Evolution, Competition, Intelligence, Identity, Eureka, Compensation

DARK

Inequality

The dark side of Victory is Inequality:

Creating disparity by being overly selfish.

Injustice, Unfair Competition, Disparity, Bias, Separation, Envy

People who have a Yellow Component contain the Elemental Energy of Victory. They are impenetrable, contradictory, and acutely aware of their emotions and intuitions. They are neither leaders nor followers—they are individuals. They crave creative control and love luxury, style, and taste. Yellows must avoid jealousy, not necessarily of others but of their place in the world. Their experience is unique and it is theirs to own and embrace.

Their worst childhood influence was that "it's not okay to feel too happy or too functional." Of course, it is quite alright to have fun while you are accomplishing things, and it is quite alright to have fun in general. Yellows fear becoming insignificant, but this will ease when they let go of their deepest belief that "you are good if you can be yourself." Yellows must learn that they do not need the approval, appreciation, or permission of anyone else in order for them to be themselves. In order to feel loved, Yellows must feel appreciated for who they are. They must find people who have an authentic understanding of what makes them truly special. Yellows can get lost in self-indulgence, not just over-eating but also self-embellishment and self-involvement. They must forget the past, and use the present as a source of renewal. Their greatest evil is disturbing the peace—"if I can't be happy, no one else can be!"

Their most important body part is the stomach. It seems that cooking, yoga, and walking about town looking at the things that they enjoy may greatly benefit Yellows.

Attributes:

- Acutely aware of their intuition
- Neither a leader, nor a follower, an individual
- True to themselves and their emotional needs
- Enjoy luxury, style, and taste
- Can spend many hours in their imaginations
- Creative and rule-breaking

Potential weaknesses:

- Impenetrable, difficult, contradictory
- Can withdraw if criticized or misunderstood
- Can feel alone, whether they are or not
- Can brood over negative emotions
- Dramatic, temperamental
- Can crumble under pressure and give up too quickly
- Want a rescuer, a protector

Must avoid:	Jealousy/envy
Worst childhood influence:	It's not okay to feel too happy or too functional.
Fears becoming:	Insignificant
Wants to be:	Appreciated for who they are
Gets lost in:	Self-indulgence
Should strive to:	Forget the past and use life as a source of renewal and growth
Greatest evil:	Creating instability/disturbing the peace
Avoid the negative of:	Red (clingy, over-involved)
Embrace the positive of:	White Color/Black Light (principled)
Deepest belief:	You are good if you can be yourself.
Body part:	Stomach

Famous people:

Lady Gaga	Jackie Kennedy Onassis	Reese Witherspoon
Albert Einstein	Ellen DeGeneres	Prince

5
Green Light & Color

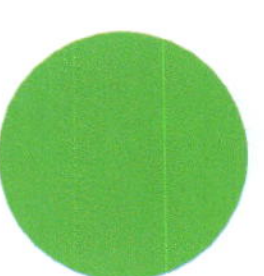

5

Deep Dive: Green Light & Color

Reason

The Elemental Energy that asserts itself when there is Green Light or Green Color is Reason.
Green Light and Green Color are comprised of:

Primary Behavior Trait: **Creativity** | Primary Comprehension Trait: **Logic**

BRIGHT

Inclusion

The bright side of Reason is Inclusion:

Treating oneself, others, and the world justly and impartially.

Discernment, Fair Competition, Patience, Decency, Civility, Veracity

DARK

Exclusion

The dark side of Reason is Exclusion:

Removing oneself, others, or ideas from consideration or privilege.

Correct & Incorrect, Rejection, Omission, Avarice, Ostracism, Greed

People with a Green Component contain the Elemental Energy of Reason. They are perceptive, innovative, and visionary and can also be quirky, unusual, or mystical. They crave privacy and stability and possess the powers of mastery and concentration. They must avoid avarice and greed. Greens sometimes keep or withhold information, resources, or themselves from others and the world.

Their worst childhood message was that "it's not okay to be comfortable." However, comfort is a vital part of life. It's where we find balance, pleasure, and restoration. You don't have to be comfortable all the time—we can grow when we are uncomfortable—but a plant that goes too long without nourishment will surely perish. Greens fear becoming useless or incompetent. This fear will be released when Greens let go of their deepest belief that "you are good if you can do something well." Greens must realize that both they and others can be good even if they cannot do anything well. In order to feel loved, Greens must feel supported. They often get lost in frivolous efforts and meaningless specializations. It turns out, you cannot actually know everything, and Greens often forget this fact. Greens must learn to be present without judgment or expectation and to stop observing the world and to start participating in it.

Their most important body part is the heart. They will benefit from walking, hiking, jogging, and push-ups. They may also benefit from pink foods like salmon, figs, and grapefruit.

Attributes:

- Perceptive, innovative, visionary
- Wise, discerning, mystical, sensitive
- Possess unique and powerful perspectives and understandings
- Can be talkative but often prefer to observe others
- Slow and meticulous workers, fine-tuners of concepts
- Wants knowledge, understanding, and expertise
- Curious, observant, a tinkerer
- Possess the power of concentration and mastery

Potential weaknesses:

- Craves privacy, stability, and trust
- Condescending, pretentious, resource-anxious
- Prefers to solve problems on their own
- Can feel small or even invisible
- Unusual, quirky, solitary, weird

Must avoid: Avarice

Worst childhood message: It's not okay to be comfortable.

Fears becoming: Useless and incompetent

Wants to be: Supported for who they are

Gets lost in: Useless specialization and frivolous efforts

Should strive to: Be engaged with themselves and the world without judgment or expectations

Greatest evil: Withholding themselves, information, or resources from others

Avoid the negative of: Purple (hyperactive, scattered)

Embrace the positive of: Pink (decisive, confident)

Deepest belief: You are good if you can do something well.

Body part: Heart

Famous people:

Barack Obama · Georgia O'Keeffe · Bill Gates

Lily Tomlin · Stephen Hawking

6
Blue Light & Color

6

Deep Dive: Blue Light & Color

Tolerance

The Elemental Energy that asserts itself when there is Blue Light or Blue Color is Tolerance.
Blue Light and Blue Color are comprised of:

Primary Behavior Trait: **Responsibility** | Primary Comprehension Trait: **Intuition**

BRIGHT

Liberty

The bright side of Tolerance is Liberty:

The right to any non-violent existence.

Choice, Decision, Personal Authority, Emancipation

DARK

Anarchy

The dark side of Tolerance is Anarchy:

Disorder resulting from a lack of external and internal control.

Imbalance, Confusion, Revolt, Impatience, Hostility

People with a Blue Component contain the Elemental Energy of Tolerance. They are engaged, responsible, and committed, but can also be anxious and self-doubting. They yearn to trust people and institutions and can be powerful advocates for change. They must avoid anxiety, being mindful to care about things, but not worry about them.

Their worst childhood message was that "it's not okay to trust yourself." Of course, it is important to trust yourself and to access the deep wisdom that lives inside your Body and Mind. Without trusting ourselves, our grounding to the Universe is shaken, leaving us mentally and physically anxious. A Blue's deepest fear is being alone without support or guidance. This fear will be lessened when they let go of their deepest belief that "you are good if you believe what is right." Blues must understand that you can believe in the "wrong" things and still be a good person. Blues often find friction in a rigid attachment to their beliefs, sometimes causing them to lose friends or lovers over insignificant disagreements. In order to feel loved, they must be made to feel safe. They should strive to be present and to trust in themselves. Blues manipulate others and themselves by only seeing the worst in things. They are often apt to point out everything that is going wrong, not everything that is going right.

Their most important body part is the lungs. It seems that running, swimming, yoga, and sex are all extra fun activities for Blues. Exercising the breath helps to restore and calm them. They may also enjoy blackberries and poppy seeds.

Attributes:

- Committed, engaged, responsible
- Enjoys "the expected" versus "the unknown"
- Know the rules but don't always follow them
- Have strong personal heroes and heroines
- Hard working and dedicated to their ambitions
- Rely on those they trust most
- Can be powerful advocates for change

Potential weaknesses:

- Yearn to trust people and institutions
- Self-critical, questioning, doubting
- Worried that mistakes will cost them their security
- Not entirely comfortable making big decisions on their own
- Their first impressions are strong and hard to change
- Anxious, suspicious, high need for security

Must avoid: Anxiety

Worst childhood influence: It's not okay to trust yourself.

Fears becoming: Alone without support or guidance

Gets lost in: Rigid attachment to their beliefs

Wants to be: Safe

Should strive to: Trust in themselves and be present

Greatest evil: Only seeing the worst in themselves, others, and the world around them

Avoid the negative of: Orange (competitive, arrogant)

Embrace the positive of: White Light/Black Color (optimistic)

Deepest belief: You are good if you believe in the right thing.

Body part: Lungs

Famous people:

Robert F. Kennedy   Princess Diana   Rush Limbaugh

7
Purple Light & Color

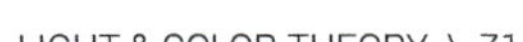

7

Deep Dive: Purple Light & Color

Peace

The Elemental Energy that asserts itself when there is Purple Light or Purple Color is Peace.
Purple Light and Purple Color are comprised of:

Primary Behavior Trait: **Confidence** | Primary Comprehension Trait: **Positivity**

BRIGHT

Joy

The bright side of Peace is Joy:

The ability to feel intense enthusiasm, interest, and self-approval.

Eagerness, Zeal, Passion, Energy, Fun

DARK

Depression

The dark side of Peace is Depression:

The internal and external loss of passion.

Misery, Dejection, Gloom, Distress, Sorrow, Melancholy

People who have Purple as one of their Components contain the Elemental Energy of Peace. People who are Purple are travelers, adventurers, and discoverers. They love languages and food, are always thinking of ten things at once, and often find themselves the center of attention. They must avoid gluttony. Essentially, they tend to overdo things.

Their worst childhood influence was that "it's not okay to rely on anyone but yourself." It is indeed okay and necessary to rely on others. Relying on others helps connect us all, and it also makes us grow when we help others in return. A Purple's deepest fear is being deprived or trapped. This will dissipate when purples let go of their deepest belief that "you are good if you get what you want." This is, of course, not true. Many people will never get what they want, and Purples must know that they and others can be perfectly good even if they do not get what they want. Purples get lost in frenetic escapism, always believing the grass will be greener on the other side. But, usually, the grass is greenest where you water it. In order to feel loved, they must feel taken care of. They are called to celebrate life and share in happiness. Their greatest evil is insisting that others meet their demands. Purples must learn that other people are still good even if those people can't live up to their specific expectations.

Their most important body part is the liver. I've often seen them benefit from foods like garlic, lemon, beets, carrots, kale, turmeric, apples, green tea, walnuts, and avocado.

Attributes:

- Traveler, adventurer, discoverer
- Enjoys excitement, variety, being busy
- Curious, unafraid to try new things
- Can see the big picture, not interested in the details
- Can almost always find a way to get what they want
- Can find themselves feeling down but bounce back
- Center of attention

Potential weaknesses:

- Scattered, comfort-seeking, thinking of ten things at once
- Can easily lose interest in or stop activities
- Easily distracted, overly indulgent, center of attention
- Can have a serious or dark side
- Cannot tolerate being bored or boring people

Must avoid: Gluttony

Worst childhood influence: It's not okay to rely on anything but yourself.

Fears becoming: Deprived and/or trapped

Gets lost in: Frenetic escapism

Wants to be: Taken care of

Should strive to: Celebrate life and share happiness

Greatest evil: Insisting that others meet their demands

Avoid the negative of: Black Light/White Color (critical)

Embrace the positive of: Green (focused, profound)

Deepest belief: You are good if you get what you want.

Body part: Liver

Famous people:

Robin Williams | Benjamin Franklin
Lucille Ball | John F. Kennedy

8
Pink Light & Color

8

Deep Dive: Pink Light & Color

Sacrifice

The Elemental Energy that asserts itself when there is Pink Light or Pink Color is Sacrifice.
Pink Light and Pink Color are comprised of:

Primary Behavior Trait: **Confidence** | Primary Comprehension Trait: **Intuition**

BRIGHT

True Love

The bright side of Sacrifice is True Love:

The ability to eternally sacrifice and forgive others and the world.

Devotion, Unconditional Love, Tenderness, Compassion

DARK

Betrayal

The dark side of Sacrifice is Betrayal:

To be unfaithful in guarding, maintaining, or honoring one's own or another's promises.

Misguide, Lust, Reject, Discourage, Exploit, Devastate

People with a Pink Light or Pink Color Component have the Elemental Energy of Sacrifice. They are strongly independent, and they hate relying on other people. They are caring and protective of those close to them, can be funny or even edgy, and they know how to get results. They must avoid lust, not just sexual lust but an obsessive or blinded approach to life.

Their worst childhood message was that "it's not okay to be vulnerable." Being vulnerable is the key to love, sexual pleasure, and experiencing a full life. It is important to be vulnerable. Their deepest fear is being harmed or controlled by others. This fear will be allayed when they let go of their deepest belief that "you are good if you are strong and in control." Pinks must learn that even when they or others are weak and out of control, they are still good people. This is the essence of true love of self and others. Pinks must stand up and fight for what they believe in. However, their greatest evil is demanding that others do as they believe. Even if you have someone's best intentions at heart, you cannot make them do as you believe.

Their most important body part is the brain. They seem to greatly benefit from playing intellectual games and reading books or watching TV shows with interesting or complex narratives. They may enjoy brain-healthy foods like salmon, potatoes, leafy greens, and fresh berries.

Attributes:

- Caring and protective of those close to them
- Knows how to get results
- Strong-willed, do not give up, do not back down
- Loves to see the people they care about succeed
- Has a tender, sensitive side they rarely share
- Believes in hard work and struggle
- Feels that life is, overall, a messy process
- Feels most alive when doing the impossible

Potential weaknesses:

- Uncomfortable with weakness or being weak
- Blunt, straightforward, crude
- Can be furious but not for too long
- Doesn't like to be last, will not lose
- Strongly independent, hates relying on others

Must avoid:	Lust
Worst childhood message:	It's not okay to be vulnerable.
Fears becoming:	Harmed or controlled by others
Gets lost in:	Endless and pointless fights
Wants to be:	Unconditionally loved
Should strive to:	Stand up for themselves and fight for what they believe in
Greatest evil:	Demanding that others do as they believe
Avoid the negative of:	Green (secretive, anxious)
Embrace the positive of:	Red (caring, open-hearted)
Deepest belief:	You are good if you are strong and in control.
Body part:	Brain
Famous people:	
Paris Hilton	Frank Sinatra
Franklin D. Roosevelt	Anne Frank

9
White Light & Black Color

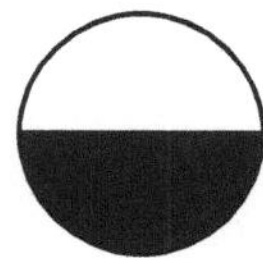

9

Deep Dive: White Light and Black Color

Acceptance

The Elemental Energy that asserts itself when there is White Light or Back Color is Acceptance.
White Light and Black Color are comprised of:

Primary Behavior Trait: **Creativity** | Primary Comprehension Trait: **Positivity**

BRIGHT

Serenity

The bright side of Acceptance is Serenity:

The ability to accept that which is unchangeable, change that which is changeable, and know the difference between the two.

Internal Peace, Patience, Assurance, Connection

DARK

Destruction

The dark side of Acceptance is Destruction:

The ultimate understanding of the finite and the fragility of existence.

Death, Hopelessness, Extinguish, Annihilation, Uselessness, Fragmentation

People with a White Light or Black Color Component contain the Elemental Energy of Acceptance. They are receptive, reassuring, and make people feel safe. They choose positivity over negativity and make long-lasting friends and partners. They must avoid sloth or being too complacent.

Their worst childhood influence was that "it's not okay to assert yourself." When people with White Light or Black Color learn to assert themselves, they can become quite powerful. They must also learn to not neglect themselves or others. Their deepest fear is becoming disconnected or destroyed. This fear will end when they let go of their deepest belief that "you are good if those around you are happy." They must learn that even if everyone around them is unhappy, they are still good people. In order to feel love, they must feel included. People with White Light or Black Color should strive to bring healing and peace into the world.

Their most important body part is the hands, so golfing, piano playing, sewing, or painting are excellent activities for them.

Attributes:

- Receptive and reassuring, makes people feel safe
- Feels comfortable with people or by themselves
- Seeks balance and simple pleasures
- Does not let things get them down easily
- Level-headed and even-keeled, persistent
- Can easily sympathize with different points of view
- Takes life as it comes
- Positivity over negativity
- Philosophical, knows how to relax

Potential weaknesses:

- Can be passive and overly agreeable
- Can appear aloof or distracted
- Apathetic and complacent
- Hard-headed, stubborn, destructive

Must avoid:	Disengagement/sloth
Worst childhood influence:	It's not okay to assert yourself.
Fears becoming:	Disconnected or destroyed
Gets lost in:	Persistent neglect
Wants to be:	Included
Should strive to:	Bring peace and healing into the world
Greatest evil:	Ignoring others and themselves
Avoid the negative of:	Blue (anxious, worried)
Embrace the positive of:	Orange (energetic, assertive, self-developing)
Deepest belief:	You are good if those around you are happy.
Body part:	Hands
Famous people:	
Janet Jackson	Abraham Lincoln
George Lucas	Alicia Keys

Summary

After examining all the Lights & Colors of our Human Universe, as well as the 3 Light & Color Components of your aura, you will now have a wide range of information to understand and internalize. Take some time to process what you've learned and enjoy the process of unraveling your thoughts without judgment. It is not important to remember everything. You can always come back to this little pink book for reminders of who you are, who you are becoming, and what will be both helpful and harmful for you along your journey. Try to hold on to the things that give you energy and relieve tension. Focus on the opportunity of understanding your full Terrestrial Vessel, both the positives and the negatives.

Chapter 8

The Light & Colour Portrait Gallery

While writing this book, I interviewed and painted 29 subjects to create a series of 18 Light & Colour Portraits. For each portrait, I would assess the subject using the Light & Color Theory Quiz, and then I would proceed to paint them a conceptual portrait based on their results.

The paintings that are composed of solid color blocks represent what the Lights and Colors of the subject's aura might feel like from far away. The paintings consisting of patterns and brush strokes represent what the subject's Lights and Colors might feel like under a microscope. The Microscope Paintings are inspired by the artwork of Sally H. Potenza, an abstract expressionist from the 60s and 70s who painted abstract representations of her cells under a microscope. The Color Blocks are inspired by architect Luis Barragán whose beautiful designs powerfully combine vibrant color, elegant modernity, and minimalism.

While painting, I tried to adhere to the principles of Impressionism, Cubism, and Abstract Expressionism. I have always been deeply impressed by the works of Claude Monet, Pablo Picasso, Jackson Pollock, Lee Krasner, and Mark Rothko and try to use inspiration from them in my paintings.

Morgen and Christina

Morgen

Mind	=	Pink Light	=	Sacrifice (Confidence + Intuition)
Body	=	Yellow Color	=	Victory (Creativity + Intuition)
Being	=	Orange Color	=	Dominance (Confidence + Logic)

Christina

Mind	=	Purple Light	=	Peace (Confidence + Positivity)
Body	=	Red Color	=	Power (Responsibility + Positivity)
Being	=	Red Color	=	Power (Responsibility + Positivity)

Morgen

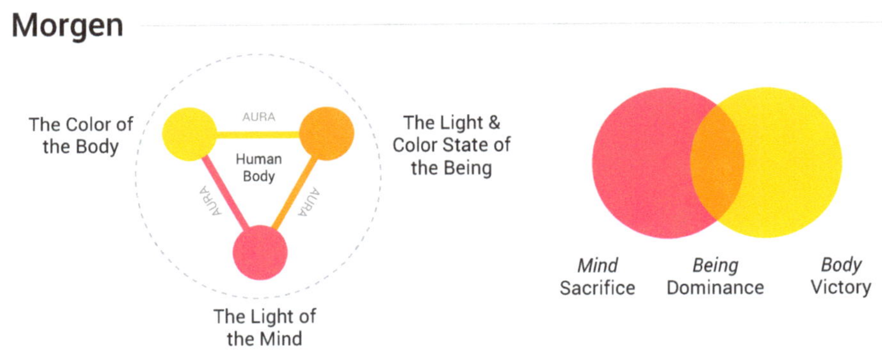

Christina

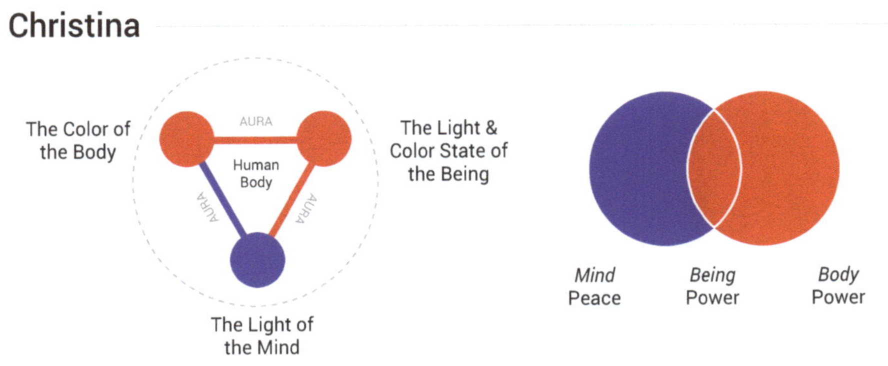

Morgen's Body is Yellow—the Light & Color of Victory. Her mind is Pink—the Light & Color of Sacrifice. When Pink Light (Sacrifice) is shined onto Yellow Color (Victory) the Light & Color State of the Being is Orange, or Dominance.

Morgen is acutely aware of her intuitions, stays true to herself, and enjoys luxury, style, and taste. She values creativity and uniqueness. She is strongly independent, and she hates relying on others. She is also highly capable of getting results and loves to see her friends and family succeed. She is funny, exciting, and extremely protective of those she loves.

Morgen glows when things are going well for her. She is efficient and effective and makes an excellent first impression. She likes to win, often at a great cost, and it's important to her to be successful. Morgen must avoid deception. Occasionally, she can be too charming and too strong-willed for her own good. She should focus on developing herself and leading through her own amazing example.

Christina's Body is Red—the Light & Color of Power. Her mind is Purple—the Light & Color of Peace. When Purple Light (Peace) is shined onto Red Color (Power), the Light & Color State of the Being is a deep Red.

Christina is friendly, talkative, and has a genuine concern for others. She expresses her emotions freely, and she is much fierier than people expect. Christina also has the ability to heal broken hearts. Both Christina's kindness and generosity have helped many people throughout the years, including myself.

Christina is also a traveler, adventurer, and discoverer. Nothing stops her from doing something fun. She loves languages and food and is always thinking of ten things at once. Christina is often at the center of attention—both intentionally and unintentionally.

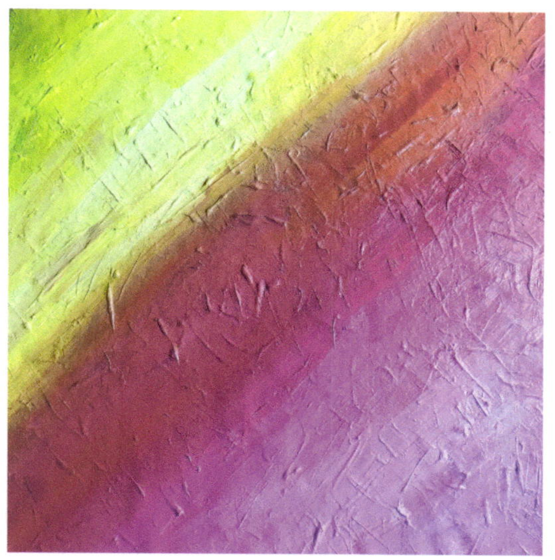

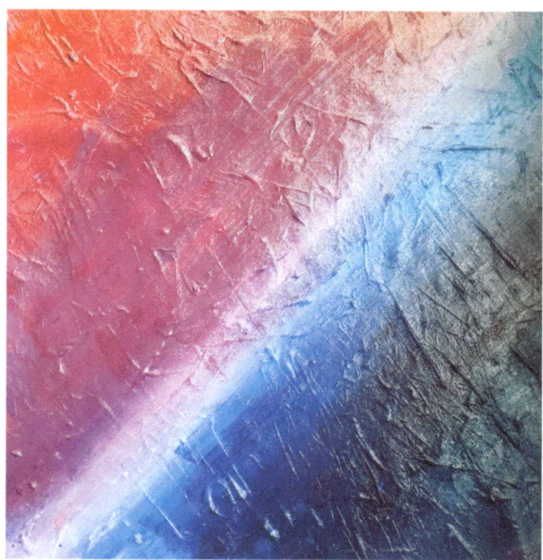

Title: *Devotion I and II*

President Barack Obama

Mind	=	Purple Light	=	Peace (Confidence + Positivity)
Body	=	Green Color	=	Reason (Creativity + Logic)
Being	=	Black Color	=	Acceptance (Creativity + Positivity)

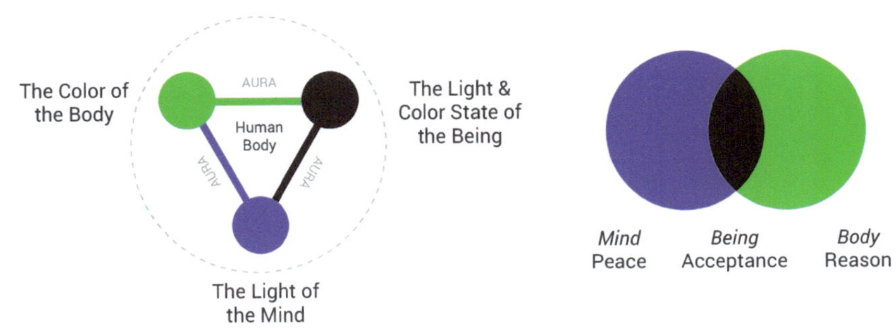

After watching President Obama's 2012 re-election campaign, I became familiar with his Light & Color Components and made the following assessment.

President Obama's Body is Green—the Light & Color of Reason. His mind is Purple—the Light & Color of Peace. When Purple Light (Peace) is shined onto Green Color (Reason) the resulting Light & Color State of the Being is Black, the color of Acceptance.

President Obama is visionary, wise, and discerning. He has unique perspectives, and he craves knowledge, intimacy, and stability. He has tremendous powers of both concentration and mastery.

President Obama is also a traveler and an adventurer. He cannot stand being bored or being with boring people. He is curious, unafraid, and he can see the big picture.

President Obama is reliable, makes people feel safe, and knows how to handle the ups and downs of the Universe. He makes for an excellent and long-lasting friend or partner. President Obama knows how to relax and philosophize. He is persistent, almost stubborn, and yet even-keeled.

Barack Obama's influence is profound, and it will unfold over many centuries. His deepest impact, perhaps, is his true significance in ushering in a new era of Reason. Human life is no longer about being best. It is about being fair. It is our highest calling right now to pursue fairness, maximize inclusion, and minimize exclusion. President Obama is the cornerstone of this transition, and it is an amazing contribution.

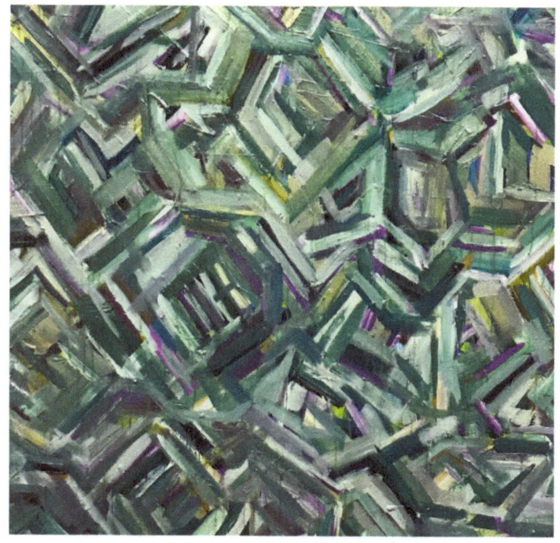

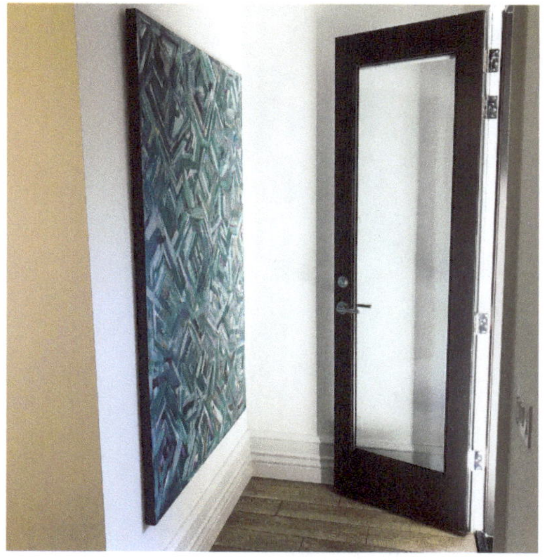

Title: *Lavender*

Lisa and William

Lisa

Mind	=	White Light	=	Acceptance (Creativity + Positivity)
Body	=	Black Color	=	Acceptance (Creativity + Positivity)
Being	=	Black Color	=	Acceptance (Creativity + Positivity)

William

Mind	=	Orange Light	=	Dominance (Confidence + Logic)
Body	=	Green Color	=	Reason (Creativity + Logic)
Being	=	Green Color	=	Reason (Creativity + Logic)

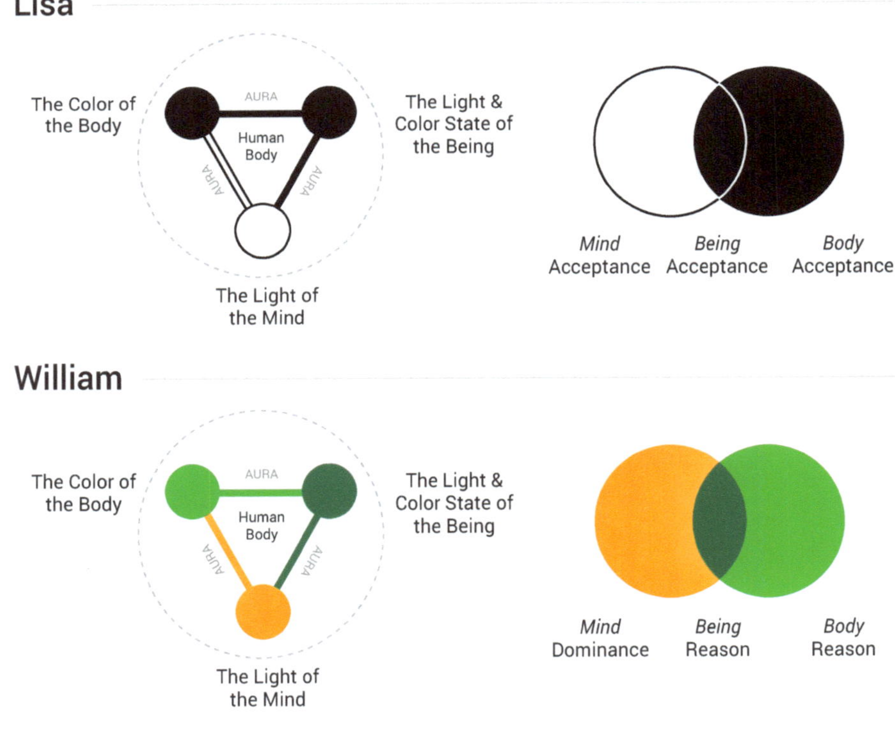

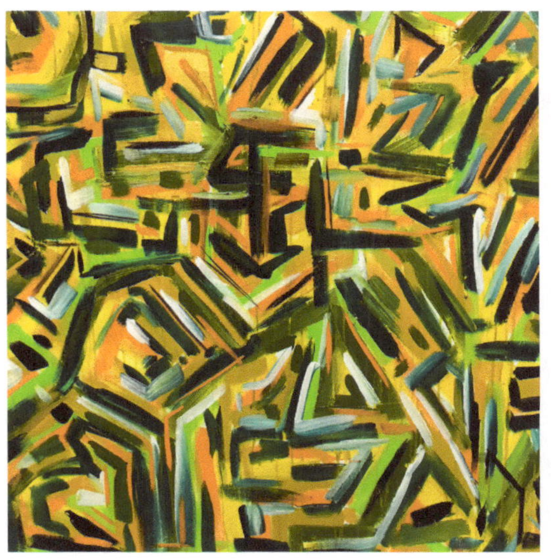

Title: *Sophistication*

Nikal and Robert

Nikal

Mind = Green Light = Reason (Creativity + Logic)
Body = Yellow Color = Victory (Creativity + Intuition)
Being = Green Color = Reason (Creativity + Logic)

Robert

Mind = Orange Light = Dominance (Confidence + Logic)
Body = Orange Color = Dominance (Confidence + Logic)
Being = Orange Color = Dominance (Confidence + Logic)

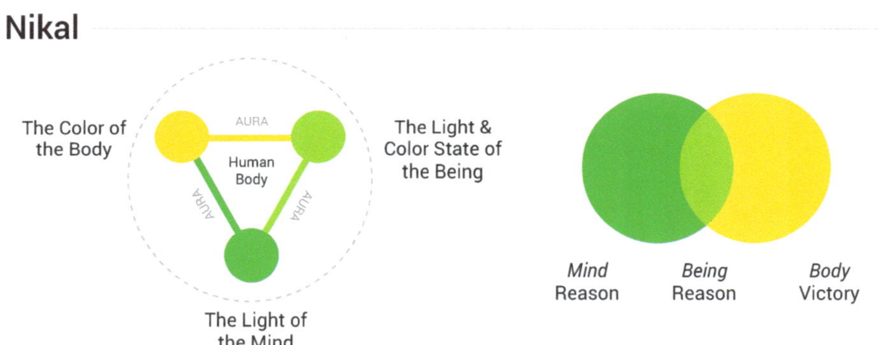

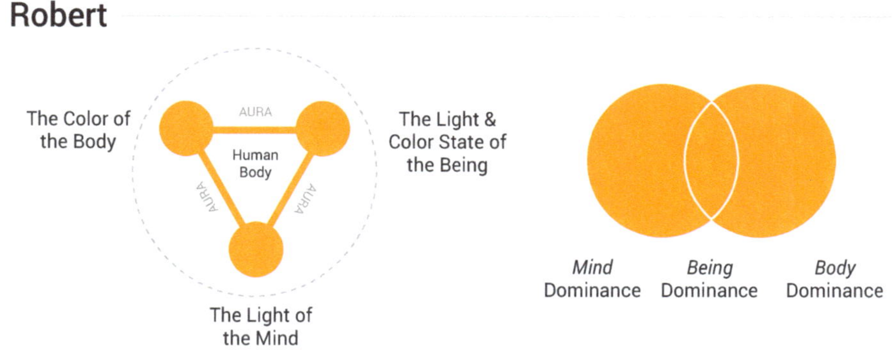

Nikal's Body is Yellow—the Light & Color of Victory. Her mind is Green—the Light & Color of Reason, making the Light & Color State of her Being, Green or one of Reason.

Nikal is deeply aware of her intuitions, and she enjoys style and taste. She is a brilliant architect and designer, a founding partner, and she received her Bachelor of Science in architecture as well as a minor in economic development. She designs some of the most elegantly conceived homes in the world. They are truly breathtaking. Nikal deeply values creativity and uniqueness, and she proceeds through life not necessarily as a leader nor as a follower but as a true individual.

Nikal is also perceptive and visionary. Her mind is powerful and she yearns for intimacy and knowledge. She has the power of mastery.

Robert's Mind, Body, and Being are all Orange—the Light & Color of Dominance.

Robert glows when things are going well for him. He is efficient and effective, and he makes an excellent first impression. He loves to win, and it's important to him to be successful. He is adaptable, goal-focused, and has achieved many big things.

Robert is a powerful entrepreneur, a founding partner, and a graduate of the United States Air Force Academy. In fact, he still exercises his flying muscles in his very own plane.

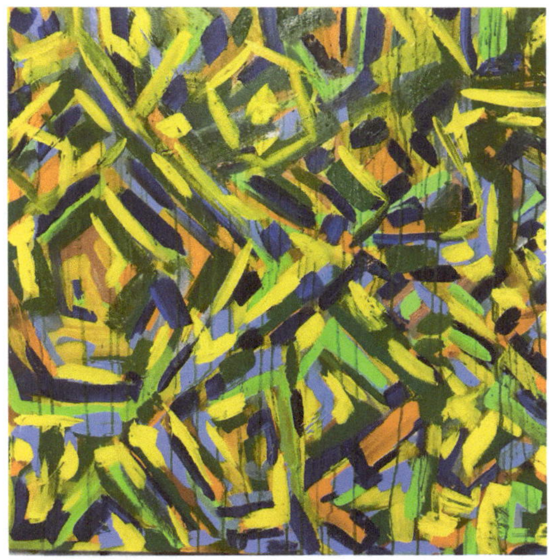

Title: *Efficiency*

Hedan and Will

Hedan

Mind = Blue Light = Tolerance (Responsibility + Intuition)
Body = Orange Color = Dominance (Confidence + Logic)
Being = Black Color = Acceptance (Creativity + Positivity)

Will

Mind = Green Light = Reason (Creativity + Logic)
Body = Purple Color = Peace (Confidence + Positivity)
Being = Black Color = Acceptance (Creativity + Positivity)

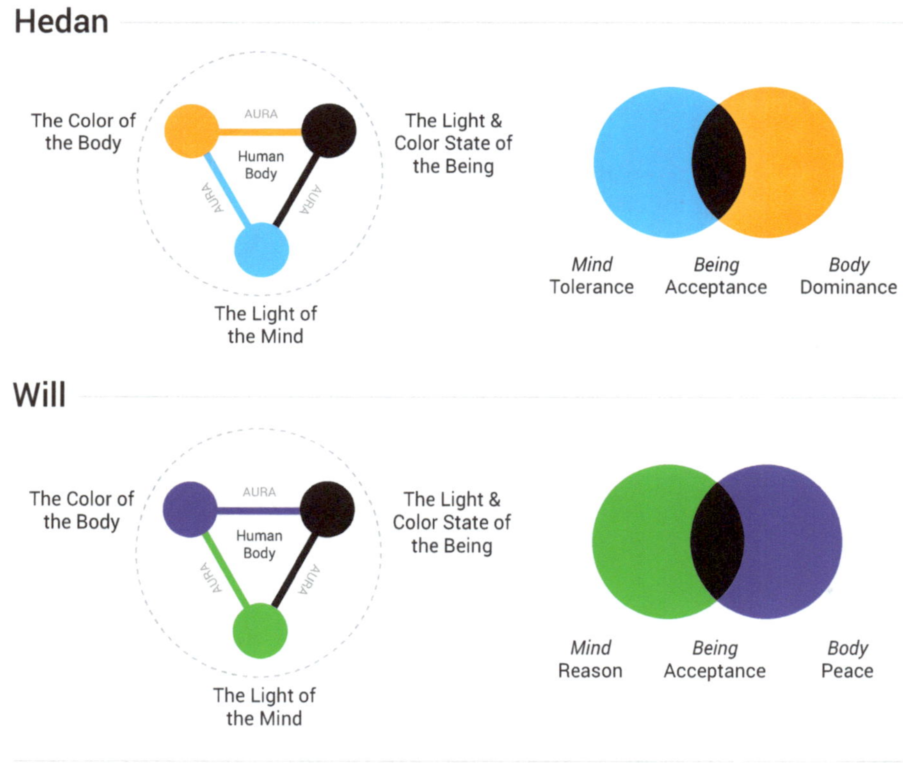

In the summer of 2018, I spent a lovely day with Will and Hedan in San Francisco. Will was my roommate at university. We lived with our fun and brilliant mathematician friend, Ashwin, in a tiny brick dormitory that was built in 1927. It was Hedan's birthday when I was visiting. Will took me out to dim sum for lunch, and then the three of us had a fabulous dinner later that evening that featured everything from smoked duck to delicious dumplings and exotic gin cocktails. It was a fantastic time. Will and Hedan were celebrating their seventh anniversary that summer. Later that week I painted their portraits.

Hedan's Body is Orange—the Light & Color of Dominance. Her Mind is Blue—the Light & Color of Tolerance, making the Light & Color State of her Being Black, the color of Acceptance.

Hedan is a product manager in Silicon Valley, California. She is a former advertising account manager, and she graduated from Columbia University. Hedan has proven to be an excellent manager, far outperforming many other people her age. She is extremely committed to her team and makes valiant efforts to do things the right way. Hedan is also an excellent conversationalist.

Will's Body is Purple—the Light & Color of Peace. His Mind is Green—the Light & Color of Reason, making his Light & Color State of the Being Black, the color of Acceptance.

After deciding to change careers, Will spent months traveling in Asia learning new culinary techniques. He is now a chef specializing in Lanzhou hand-pulled noodles and wok at a Michelin star restaurant in San Francisco, California. He is curious, unafraid, and usually capable of getting what he wants in life. Will can cook, compose, and discuss philosophy. He's a wonderfully talented person.

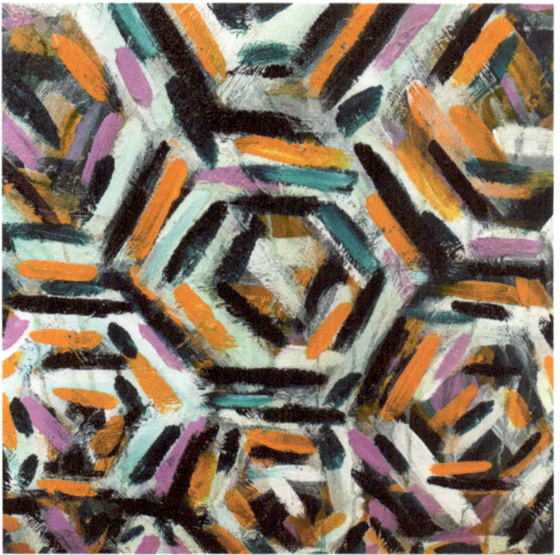

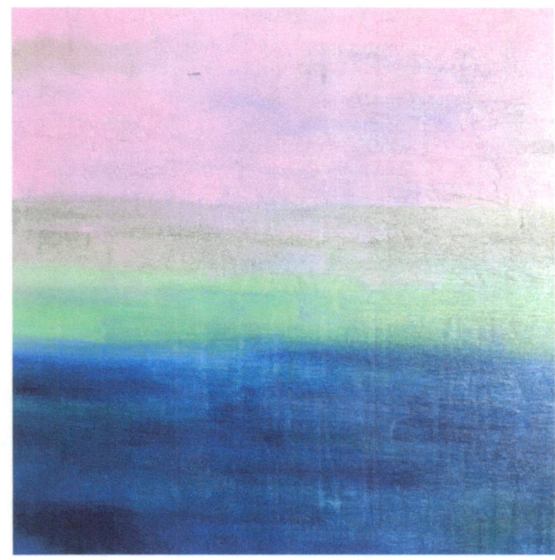

Title: *Bird of Paradise*

Tracey and Pete

Tracey

Mind = Blue Light = Tolerance (Responsibility + Intuition)
Body = Red Color = Power (Responsibility + Positivity)
Being = Black Color = Acceptance (Creativity + Positivity)

Pete

Mind = Pink Light = Sacrifice (Confidence + Intuition)
Body = Red Color = Power (Responsibility + Positivity)
Being = Red Color = Power (Responsibility + Positivity)

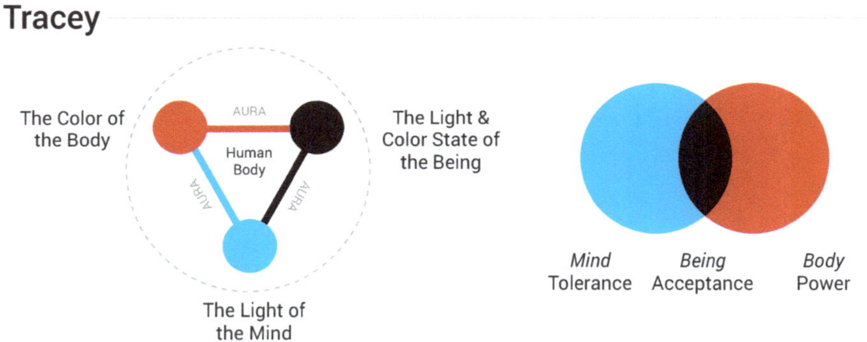

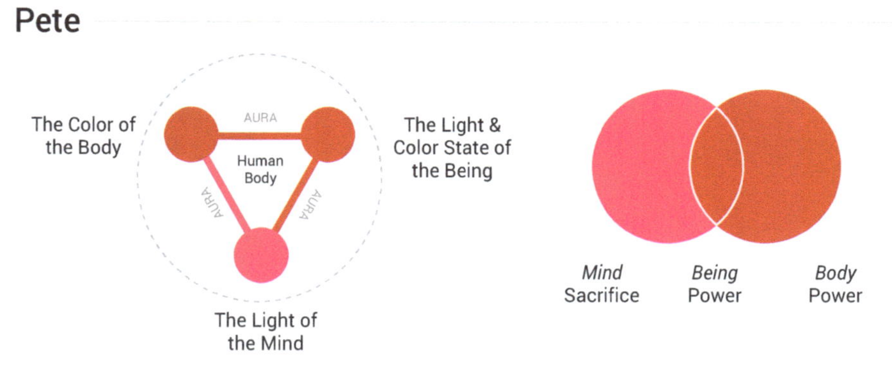

Tracey and Pete came to see me in Portland from Phoenix, Arizona. We had a great time visiting the tea garden, the rose garden, and strolling through the gently sloping streets of Portland. After their visit, I painted their Lights & Colors.

Tracey's Body is Red—the Light & Color of Power. Her Mind is Blue—the Light & Color of Tolerance, making the Light & Color State of her Being Black, or Acceptance.

Tracey is a top real estate agent and easily connects with all sorts of people. She is incredibly engaged, committed, and responsible. Tracey is always booked from morning until night. Whether it's work, friends, or family, Tracey is never without a happy commitment. Tracey is also one of the most reliable people I know.

Pete's Body is Red—the Light & Color of Power. His Mind is Pink—the Light & Color of Sacrifice. Red Color plus Pink Light creates a deep Red, making Pete's overall Light & Color State of the Being Red, or Power.

Pete is always looking out for others, and he has been a great mentor to many, many people. He is funny, exciting, and very protective of those he loves. He is also very good at getting results.

I've been lucky to be close with Tracey and Pete for over twenty years.

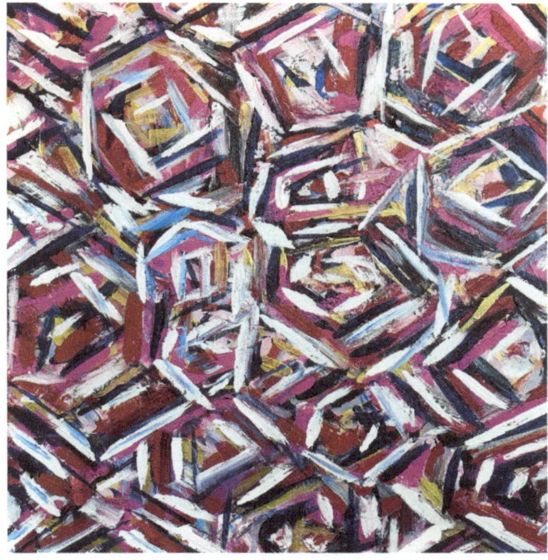

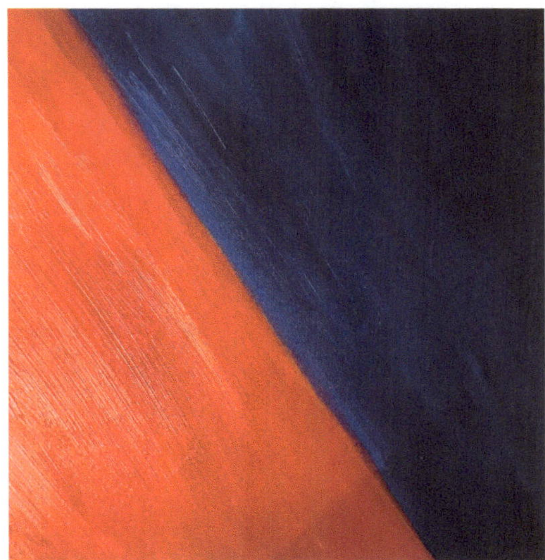

Title: *Eureka*

Akiyo

Mind = White Light = Acceptance (Creativity + Positivity)
Body = Purple Color = Peace (Confidence + Positivity)
Being = Purple Color = Peace (Confidence + Positivity)

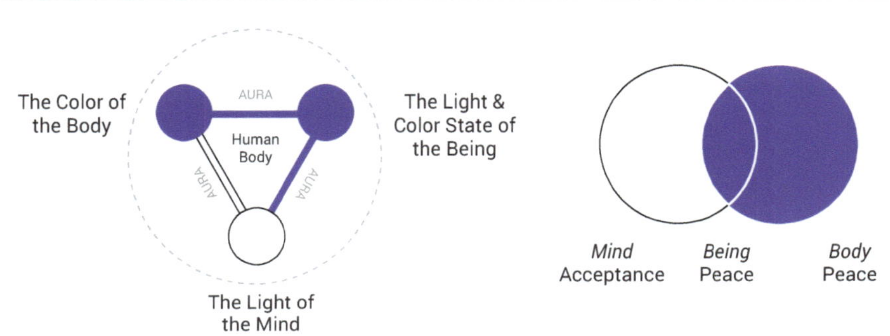

Akiyo's Body is Purple—the Light & Color of Peace. Her Mind is White—the Light & Color of Acceptance, making the Light & Color State of the Being Purple, the color of Peace.

Akiyo is my Bowen therapist from San Francisco and also a wonderful friend. She has helped me to relieve back pain for many years. She has a Purple Body and a Mind of White Light. She truly embodies Peace and Acceptance to me. Her hands are capable of deep and meaningful healing.

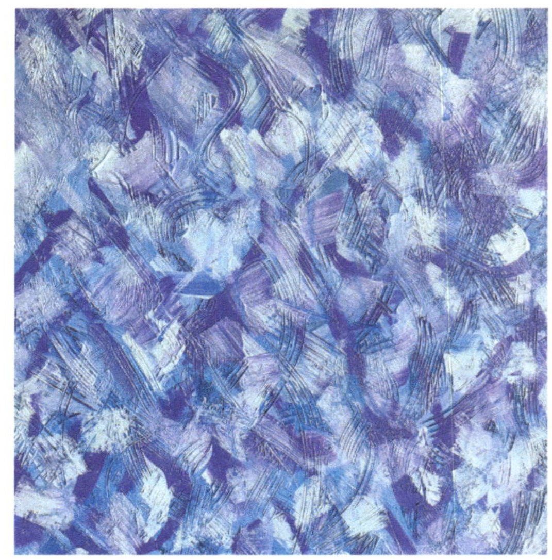

Title: *Savior*

Katerina

Mind = Purple Light = Peace (Confidence + Positivity)
Body = Yellow Color = Victory (Creativity + Intuition)
Being = Red Color = Power (Responsibility + Positivity)

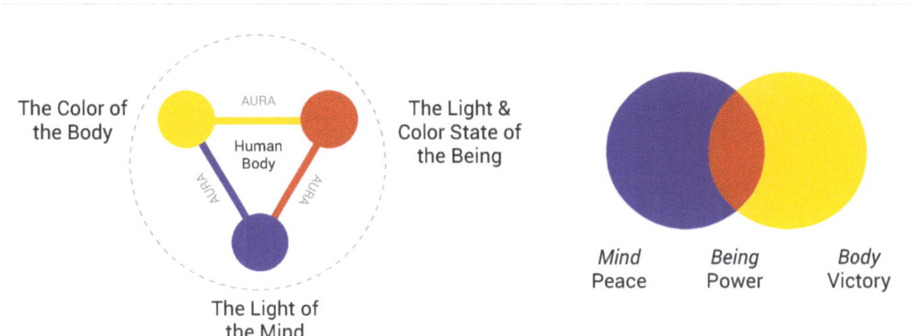

Katerina's Body is Yellow—the Light & Color of Victory. Her Mind is Purple—the Light & Color of Peace, making her Light & Color State of the Being Red, the color of Power.

Katerina is an entrepreneur, marketer, product manager, and musician. She graduated from Cornell University with a degree in music and English. Kat is an adventurer. She can't stand being bored, and she is often at the center of attention. She has a genuine concern for others and is fierier than people expect. She also loves style. I've known Kat for over five years, and she is an extraordinarily talented and ambitious person. She is also extremely kind.

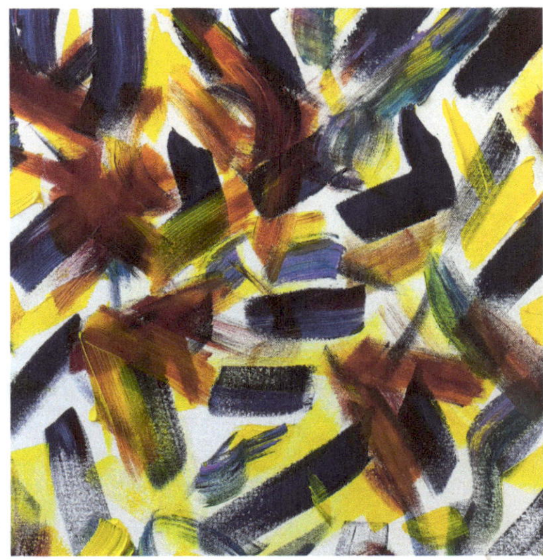

Title: *Phoenix*

Amy

Mind = Green Light = Reason (Creativity + Logic)
Body = Orange Color = Dominance (Confidence + Logic)
Being = Green Color = Reason (Creativity + Logic)

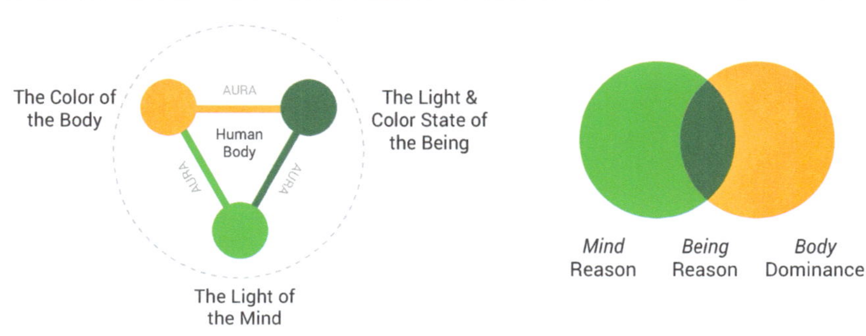

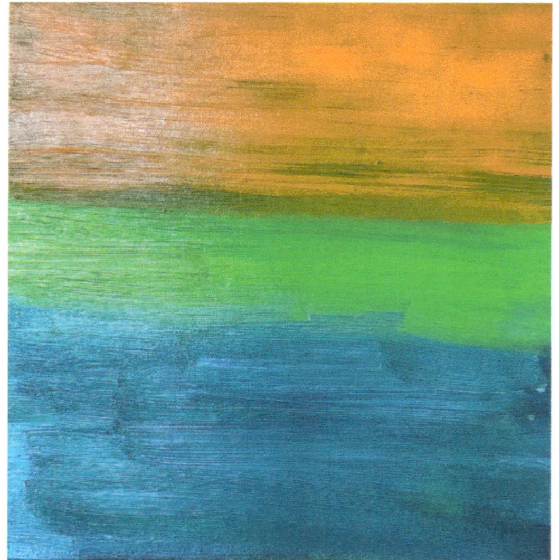

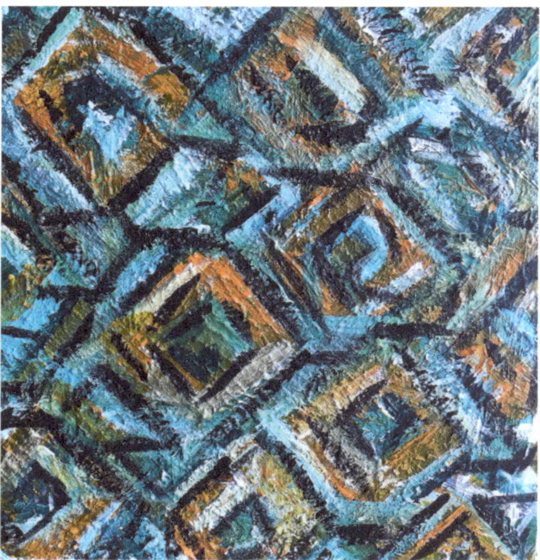

Title: *Fireflower*

Laura

Mind	=	Red Light	=	Power (Responsibility + Positivity)
Body	=	Red Color	=	Power (Responsibility + Positivity)
Being	=	Red Color	=	Power (Responsibility + Positivity)

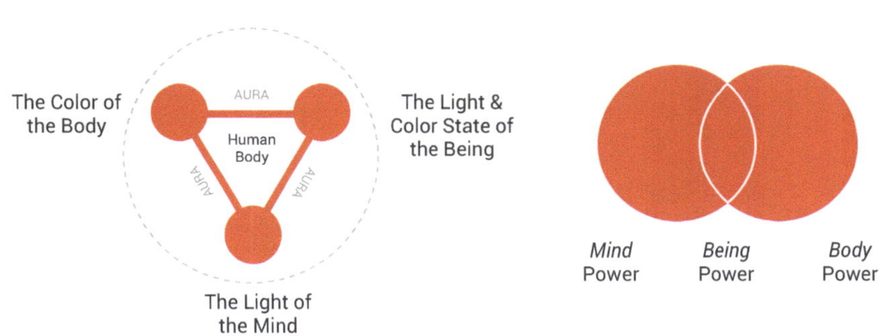

Laura's Body, Mind, and Being are all Red—the Light & Color of Power.

Laura is a practicing lawyer in New York City. She was my orientation leader at university. She is fierce, intelligent, responsible, engaged, funny, and fun. Some of my favorite school memories are of us having lunches together, discussing random topics, including politics and class-scheduling strategies.

Laura embodies the quote "speak softly and carry a big stick." Her stick, of course, is a metaphorical one. I believe that one day Laura will be one of the most powerful individuals on the planet. Her color is perfect for that too. In a lovely twist, her full name means "victory" and "peace", which in Light & Color Theory gives us Power—Red Light and Red Color.

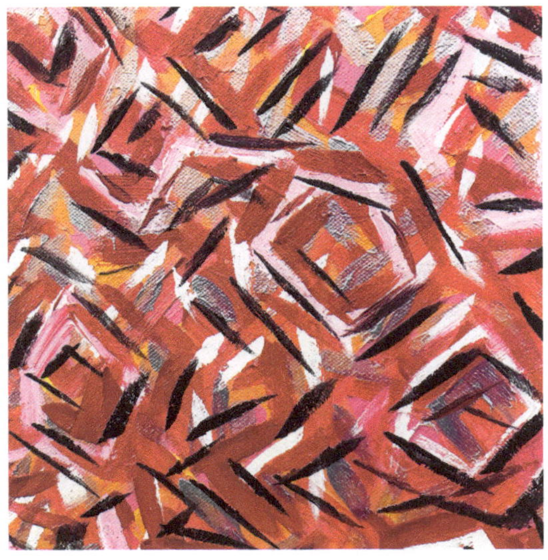

Title: *Warrior*

Keren

Mind = Pink Light = Sacrifice (Confidence + Intuition)
Body = Yellow Color = Victory (Creativity + Intuition)
Being = Orange Color = Dominance (Confidence + Logic)

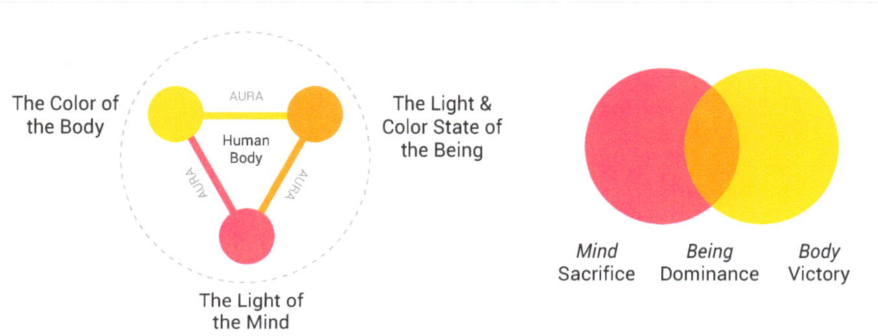

Keren's Body is Yellow—the Light & Color of Victory. Her Mind is Pink—the Light & Color of Sacrifice, making her Light & Color State of the Being Orange, the color of Dominance.

Keren is a product manager, marketer, and community leader currently working as a senior product manager in Silicon Valley. She received her BA in economics and social history from Barnard College.

Keren was the first person I would see at my work. She was impressive, fun, and extraordinarily intelligent. She was always shining. She dances, sings, plays music, creatively solves problems, and she loves doing things in unique and magical ways. She advocates for equality with her voice and her actions, and she will undoubtedly play not only a huge role in Silicon Valley but in the future of the world.

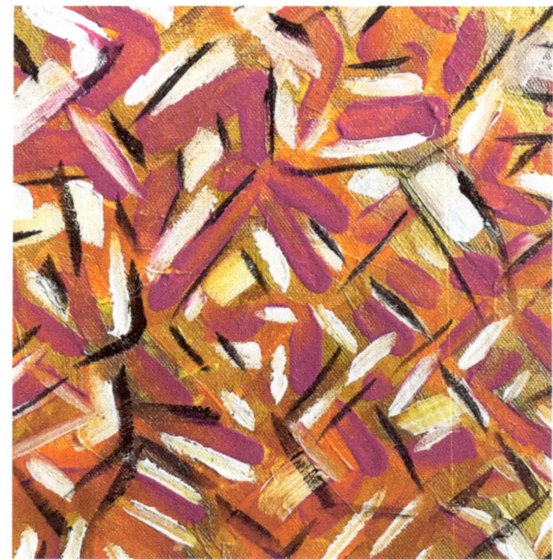

Title: *Morning Glory*

Marisa

Mind = Blue Light = Tolerance (Responsibility + Intuition)
Body = Purple Color = Peace (Confidence + Positivity)
Being = Blue Color = Tolerance (Responsibility + Intuition)

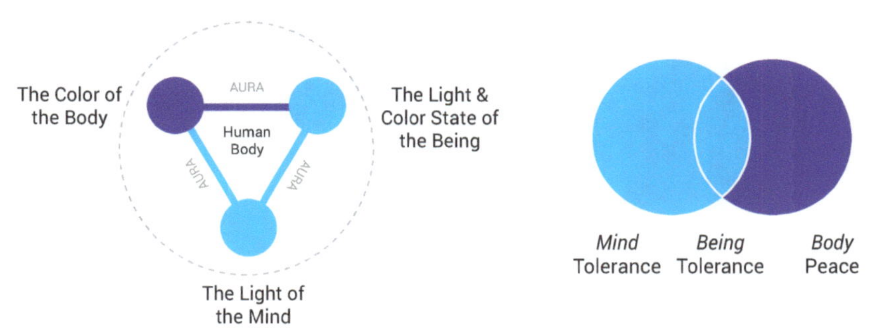

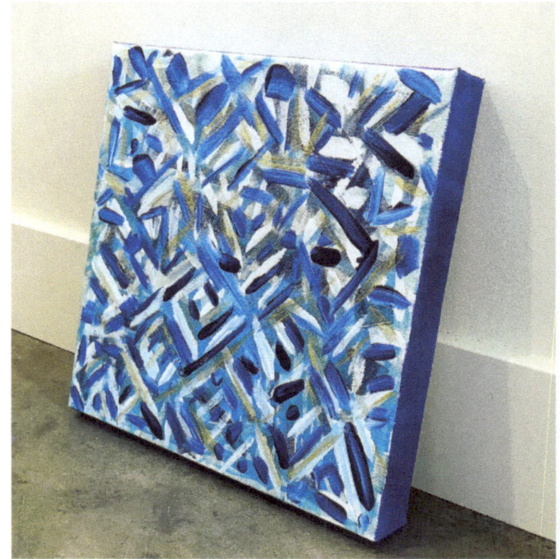

Title: *Deepest Blue*

Nicole and George

Nicole

Mind	=	Black Light	=	Instinct (Responsibility + Logic)
Body	=	Purple Color	=	Peace (Confidence + Positivity)
Being	=	Black Light	=	Instinct (Responsibility + Logic)

George

Mind	=	White Light	=	Acceptance (Creativity + Positivity)
Body	=	Black Color	=	Acceptance (Creativity + Positivity)
Being	=	Black Color	=	Acceptance (Creativity + Positivity

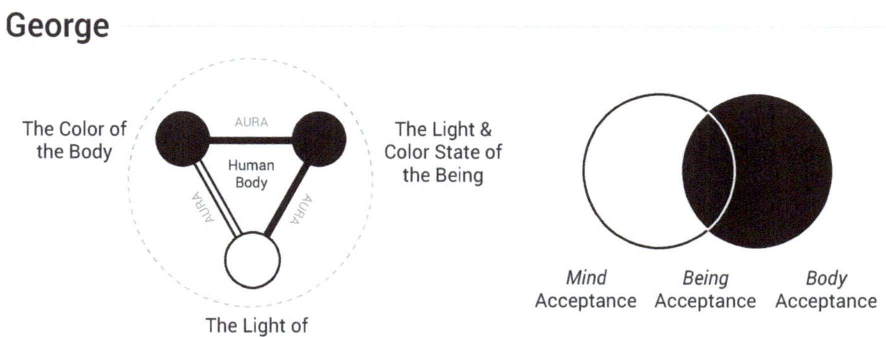

Nicole's Body is Purple—the Light & Color of Peace. Her Mind is Black Light—the Light of Instinct, making her overall Light & Color State of the Being one of Black Light.

Nicole was a flight attendant for Air Canada for many years. She is curious and unafraid to try new things. She enjoys excitement and variety. She can feel down but usually bounces back. Nicole is also a serious no-nonsense person who is honest, objective, and conscience-oriented. She believes in being better safe than sorry, and she dislikes making mistakes. She is inspired by principles and ideals and is highly organized and responsible. Sometimes she can feel overly burdened, but she likes having fun and should do it more often. She must avoid anger and enjoy living for her greater purpose. For Nicole, I would recommend foot massages and pedicures, liver detoxes, and liver healthy foods like garlic, lemon, beets, carrots, kale, turmeric, apples, green tea, walnuts, and avocado, as well as "body weight only" squats with stretching and massaging of the hamstrings and calves.

George's Body is Black, the Color of Acceptance and his Mind is White, the Light of Acceptance, making his Light & Color State of the Being Black Color.

George is receptive, reassuring, and he has the power to make people feel safe. He is level-headed, slightly stubborn, and he makes for a long-lasting friend and partner. George must avoid apathy and be sure not to ignore himself, others, or the world. His major calling is to bring peace into the world. His most important body part is the hands, and for love, he must feel included.

For George, I would recommend hand massages and manicures with regular putting, chipping, and pitching practice for hand strengthening. I've known George and Nicole for over twenty years. They are truly wonderful people.

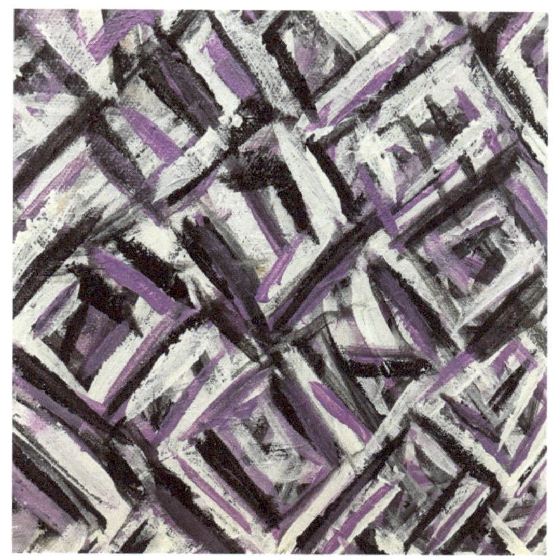

Title: *Purple Absolution*

Jessie and Thomas

Jessie

Mind = Black Light = Instinct (Responsibility + Logic)
Body = Pink Color = Sacrifice (Confidence + Intuition)
Being = Black Light = Instinct (Responsibility + Logic)

Thomas

Mind = Red Light = Power (Responsibility + Positivity)
Body = Blue Color = Tolerance (Responsibility + Intuition)
Being = Black Color = Acceptance (Creativity + Positivity)

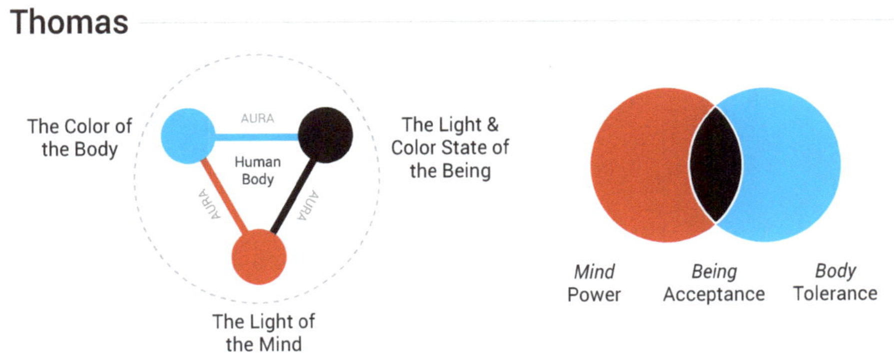

Jessie's Mind is Black Light—the Light of Instinct. Her body is Pink—the Light & Color of Sacrifice, making her overall Light & Color State of the Being Black Light.

Jessie is a no-nonsense person who is conscience-oriented. She strives for a higher purpose and hates making mistakes. She is highly responsible but knows how to have fun too. One of her most important body parts is the feet. She greatly benefits from walking on soft surfaces like beaches, golf courses, and hiking trails through the woods.

Jessie is also strongly independent and doesn't enjoy relying on others. She is caring and protective of those she is close to. She is also very funny. Her other most important body part is the brain. She benefits from playing intellectual games, reading books, or watching TV shows with interesting or complex narratives.

Thomas's Body is Blue—the Light & Color of Tolerance. His Mind is Red—the Light & Color of Power. Red Light plus Blue Color creates a Black Color Light & Color State of the Being.

Thomas is engaged, responsible, and committed. But he can also be anxious. He likes to trust in people and institutions, and he can be a powerful advocate for change. Thomas is very dedicated to his ambitions. He is a tremendous athlete. An important body for Thomas is the lungs. Things like yoga, running, and swimming help to calm him down and restore him. Thomas must avoid anxiety and should learn to trust himself and be present. He has good intuition. Thomas is also friendly and talkative. He expresses his frustrations freely, and he is fierier than people expect. He makes for a long-lasting friend.

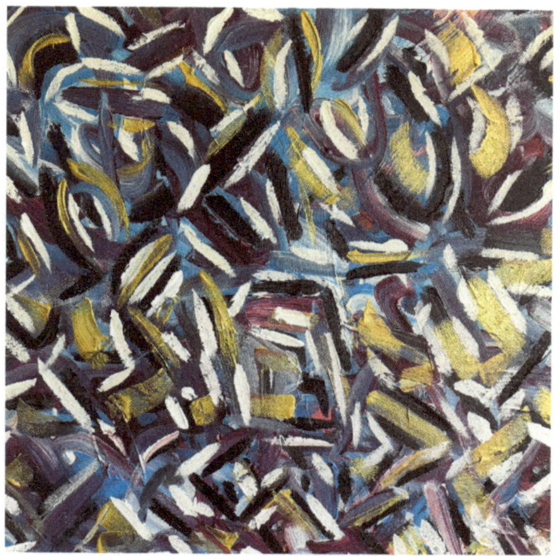

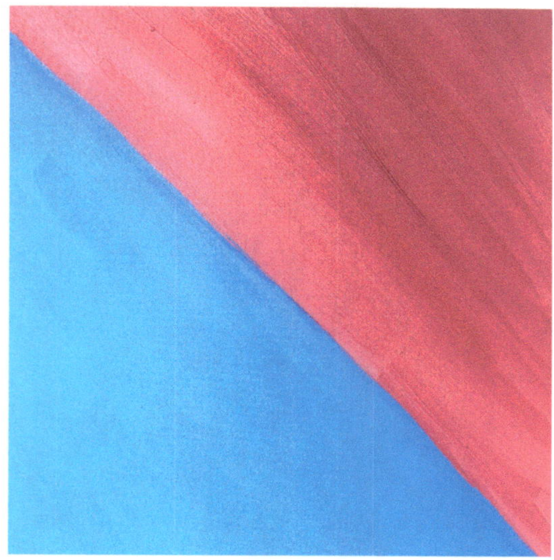

Title: *Liberty*

Allison, Rich, Graham & Carson

Allison

Mind	=	Purple Light	=	Peace (Confidence + Positivity)
Body	=	Red Color	=	Power (Responsibility + Positivity)
Being	=	Red Color	=	Power (Responsibility + Positivity)

Rich

Mind	=	Black Light	=	Instinct (Responsibility + Logic)
Body	=	Blue Color	=	Tolerance (Responsibility + Intuition)
Being	=	Black Light	=	Instinct (Responsibility + Logic)

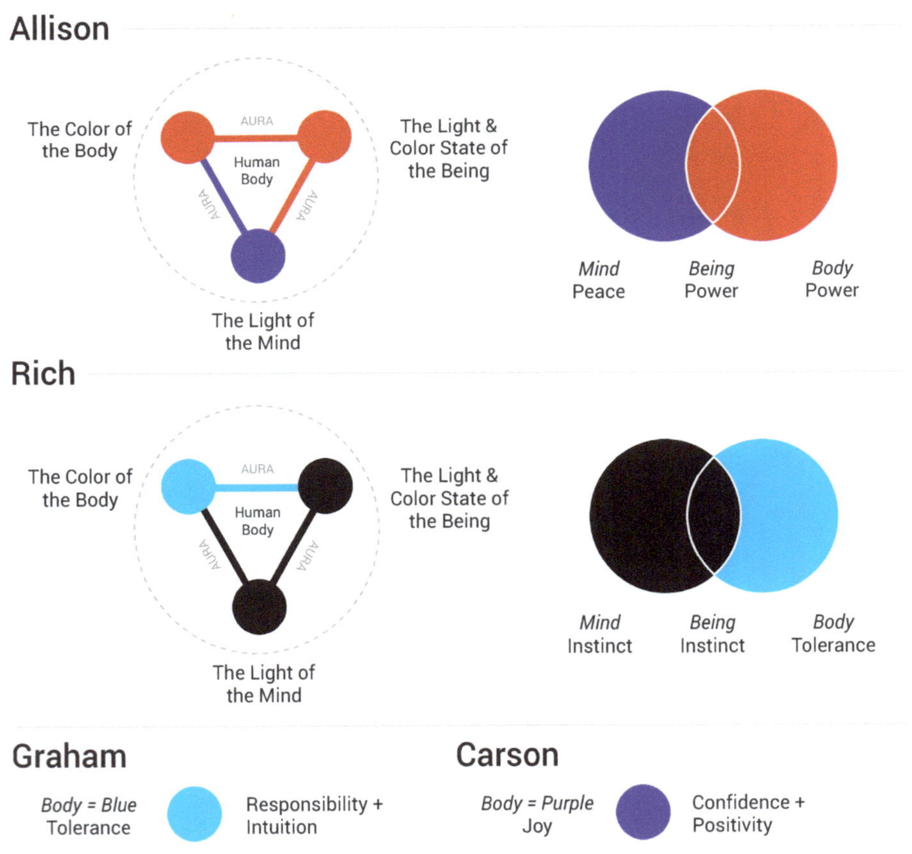

Allison was one of my first managers at work. She was vibrant, fun, hardworking, and curious. She stood out everywhere she went. She is fiercely competent and fiercely sincere. She never let anyone feel alone, and she was always willing to help, even at a great cost to herself. She worked late into the night many, many times to pull off remarkable feats.

My belief is that her two young sons, Graham and Carson, will at some point love the Superman comics. Superman, of course, is the person who their mom most resembles.

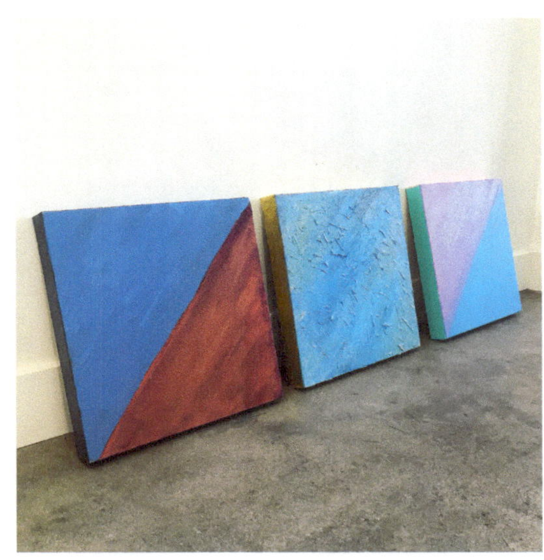

Title: *Del Mar*

Nicole

Mind = Pink Light = Sacrifice (Confidence + Intuition)
Body = Yellow Color = Victory (Creativity + Intuition)
Being = Orange Color = Dominance (Confidence + Logic)

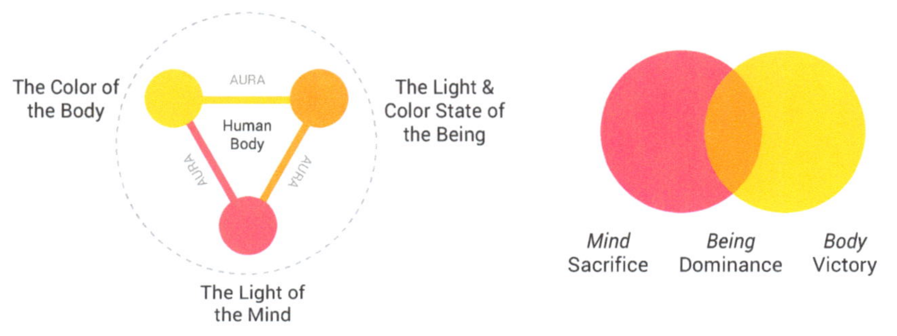

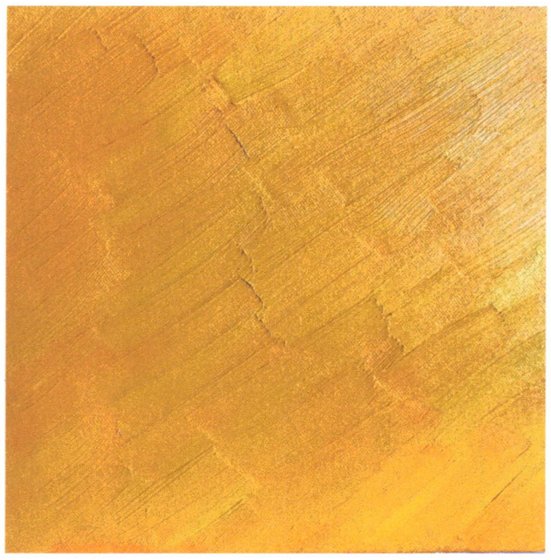

Title: *Vintage Orange*

Ryan

Mind = Pink Light = Sacrifice (Confidence + Intuition)
Body = Green Color = Reason (Creativity + Logic)
Being = Green Color = Reason (Creativity + Logic)

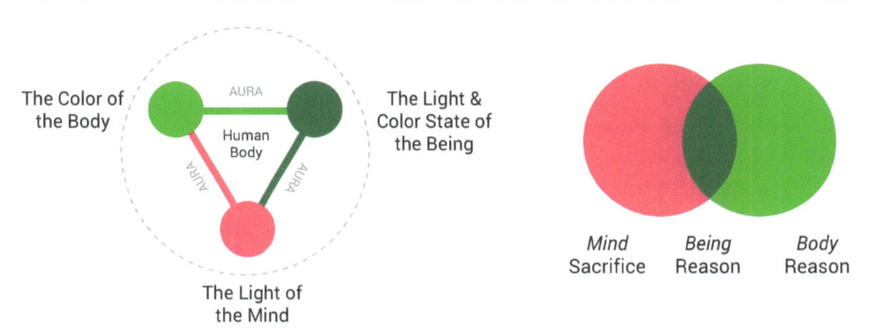

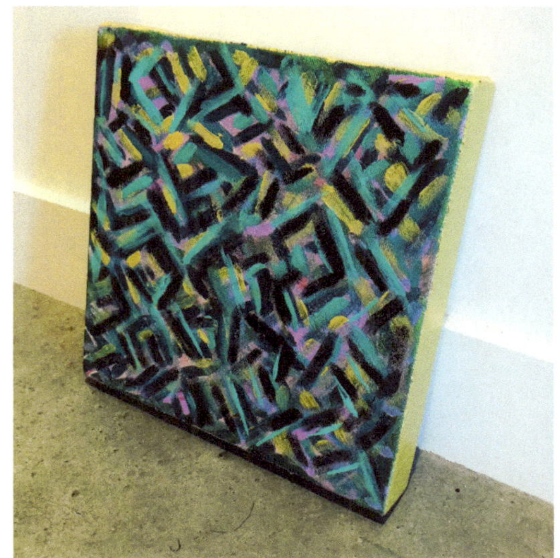

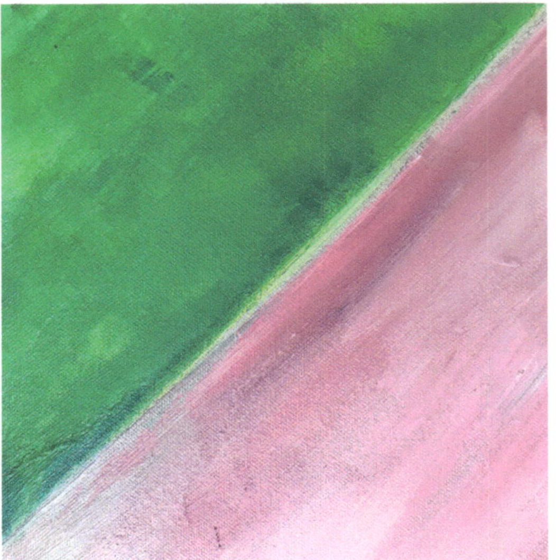

Title: *Rose*

Human Rights Campaign: Bill & Tivo

In August of 2019, I was fortunate enough to have a Light & Colour Portrait Sitting included in the Human Rights Campaign Auction in Portland, Oregon. Bill and Tivo were generous enough to buy the sitting.

Bill's Mind is Orange Light, the Light & Color of Dominance. His Body is Yellow Color, the Light & Color of Victory. Therefore his Light & Color State of the Being is Orange Color, the Color of Dominance. Tivo's Mind is also Orange Light, the Light & Color of Dominance. His Body is All Color, or Black, the Color of Acceptance. Therefore his Light & Color State of the Being is also All Color, or Black, the Color of Acceptance.

Bill and Tivo are creative, hardworking, and loving. They are kind, welcoming, and patient. It was a true pleasure to meet with them, to see their beautiful home, and view their wonderful collection of artwork. The peaceful afternoon with them reminded me of Hawaii and the beautiful hibiscus that can be seen there.

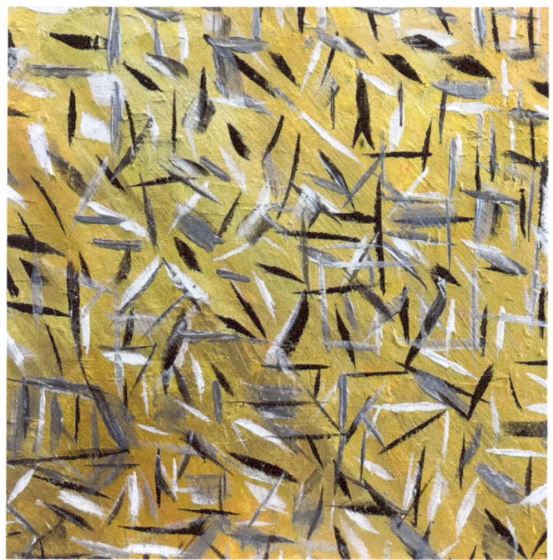

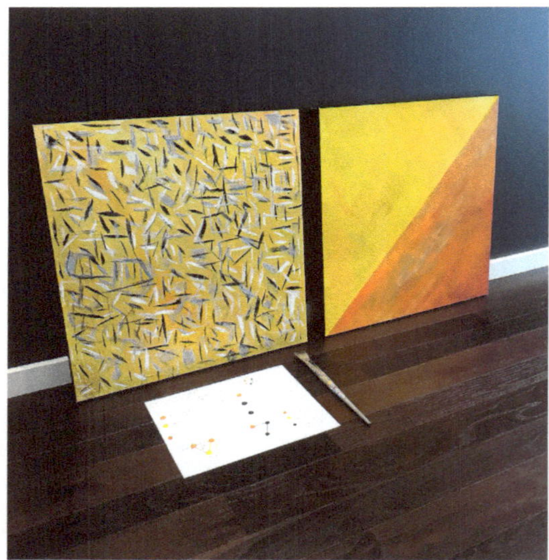

Title: *Hawaiian Hibiscus*

Chapter 9

Conclusion

After examining all the Lights & Colors of our Human Universe, as well as the 3 Light & Color Components of your aura, you have a lot of information to digest. As I said earlier, take some time to reflect on what you've learned. Feel free to enjoy the process of unraveling your thoughts without judgment. It's not about remembering every last detail. You can always come back to this book to be reminded of who you are, who you are becoming, and the things that will be helpful and harmful to you along your journey. Strive to hold on to the things that give you energy and relieve stress. Focus on the opportunity to understand both the positives and the negatives of your Human Body, your Terrestrial Vessel.

Light & Color Theory, at its core, provides a truly fundamental understanding of the Human Universe. It is a Tinkertoy that shines light onto the dynamics of power and reason, tolerance and victory, as well as on survival and acceptance. It articulates the values of achievement, victory, and liberty, while warning us of the tyrannies of oppression, inequality, and anarchy. It allows us to face our deepest fears, change our weakest beliefs, and enables us to embrace our inner and outer gifts. It can help illuminate other people's perspectives, desires, and motivations, while helping us to graciously connect with our friends, family, and lovers. Light & Color Theory inspires painting, drawing, photography, music, writing, and much more. I hope it has been a dynamic and compelling experience for you, and I hope it is an experience you will enjoy sharing with others.

Now it's simply time to enjoy the Light. Our position in space and time are mathematically, scientifically, and spiritually miraculous. Never forget to take advantage of it.

Glossary

Aura – The forces of Light and Color surrounding the Human Body. It contains 3 distinct components, all acting as one: The Light of the Mind, the Color of the Body, and the Light & Color State of the Being. Each of the 3 components affect the ways humans behave in and perceive the world around them.

Color – The filtered reflection of Light.

Conceptual Art Piece – Value is rarely found in the lines, but always found in between them.

Elemental Energy – Building block of the Human Universe.

Human Body – The Terrestrial Vessel of a Human. It is comprised of three distinct components acting as one: (Physical Mind) + (Physical Body) + (Physical Being).

Human Body Light & Color Composition – The geometric representation of the Human Body and the Lights & Colors of an aura.

Light – The light of the sun and all its components.

Light & Color Component – The Light of the Mind, The Color of the Body, or the Light & Color State of the Being. They all work together to form the aura.

Light & Color State of the Being – The state arising from the Light of the Mind shining onto the Color of the Body.

Primary Behavior Trait – Fundamental Way of Behavior (Interacting).

Primary Comprehension Trait – Fundamental Way of Comprehension (Learning).

Terrestrial Being – The Physical Mind examined in conjunction with the Physical Body, or (Thought x Action) - Behaviors in the Terrestrial Plane.

Terrestrial Body – Actions in the Terrestrial Plane.

Terrestrial Mind – Thoughts in the Terrestrial Plane.

Terrestrial Vessel – Currently, the Human Body. It is the physical vehicle with which our Celestial Vessel has chosen to experience the Earthly Plane.

Light & Color Reference Chart

Light/Color	Primary Behavior	Primary Comprehension	Elemental Energy	Polarities	Enneagram	Chakra	Sin	Body Part
Black/White	Responsibility	Logic	Instinct	Survival/ Violence	1	Earth Chakra	Wrath	Feet
Red	Responsibility	Positivity	Power	Give/ Take	2	Root Chakra	Pride	Coccyx
Orange	Confidence	Logic	Dominance	Achievement/ Oppression	3	Sacrum Chakra	Vanity/ Deception	Hips
Yellow	Creativity	Intuition	Victory	Individualism/ Inequality	4	Solar Plexus Chakra	Envy	Stomach
Green	Creativity	Logic	Reason	Inclusion/Exclu-sion	5	Heart Chakra	Avarice	Heart
Blue	Responsibility	Intuition	Tolerance	Liberty/ Anarchy	6	Throat Chakra	Sadness/Anxiety	Lungs
Purple	Confidence	Positivity	Peace	Joy/ Depression	7	Third Eye Chakra	Gluttony	Liver
Pink	Confidence	Intuition	Sacrifice	True Love/ Betrayal	8	Crown Chakra	Lust	Brain
White/Black	Creativity	Positivity	Acceptance	Serenity/ Destruction	9	Heaven Chakra	Sloth	Hands

Light & Color RGB (Red, Green, Blue) Reference Chart

The chart below illustrates the official RGB locations used for the creation of Light & Color Theory. These RGB locations indicate the levels of Red, Green, and Blue that each Light contains and are used when determining the Light & Color State of the Being.

Black Light	0,0,0,
Red	255,0,0
Orange	255,165,0
Yellow	255,255,0
Green	0,255,0
Blue	0,0,255
Purple	128,0,128
Pink	238,130,238
White Light	255,255,255

www.ingramcontent.com/pod-product-compliance
Lightning Source LLC
LaVergne TN
LVHW070127110826
845147LV00002B/199

* 9 7 8 1 6 4 1 8 4 2 2 6 6 *